THE CELTIC HEART

Tom Davies, a Welshman born and bred, trained as a journalist with *The Western Mail* and later worked for *The Sunday Times*, *The Sunday Telegraph* and *The Observer*, where for three years he was the diarist Pendennis. Now a full-time writer, he has written eleven books and his *Merlyn the Magician & the Pacific Coast Highway* was short-listed for the Thomas Cook Travel Book of the Year Award, while his pilgrimage narrative *Stained Glass Hours* won the Winifred Mary Stanford prize for the best book with a religious theme. He lives in a coast-guard tower overlooking the Bristol Channel in Penarth, South Wales and is married with three sons.

D1100934

Also by Tom Davies and published by Triangle

Landscapes of Glory (1996)

The
Celtic Heart

Tom Davies

TRIANGLE

First published in Great Britain 1997
Triangle Books
Holy Trinity Church
Marylebone Road
London NW1 4DU

British Library Cataloguing-in-Publication Data

A catalogue record of this book is available
from the British Library

ISBN 0-281-05028-7

Typeset by Pioneer Associates, Perthshire
Printed in Great Britain by
Biddles Ltd, Guildford & King's Lynn

Contents

1   Dancing in Dingle   1

2   Lost in Snowdonia   16

3   A Keening in Dunblane   28

4   Balor in Bog of Allen   41

5   A Mad Blonde at St David's   59

6   A Gunman on Skye   75

7   The Dogs of the Liffey   94

8   Visions of Hell in Ulster   118

1

Dancing in Dingle

AS MORNINGS WENT this was the lowest of the low. It had been a night of storms on the Swansea to Cork ferry and I had driven down the clattering ramps into Ireland still feeling a deep green. Now it was raining as I finally managed to find my way out of the maze that is Cork's one-way traffic system and everything was so misty and damp I could barely make out one side of the road from the other as I headed west. Neither was this queasy insecurity much helped by many of the road signs which just seemed to point straight up into the air.

Somehow I was going to have to use this rainy morning in the ancient kingdom of Kerry as the starting block from which to mount a book about the Celts. I was about to begin an investigation into what it meant to be a Celt. Whole centuries were about to fall away as my fearless questions discovered long-hidden truths in these damp, twisting, fuschia lanes. But the only question on my mind at that minute was where I might get a few aspirin.

I headed down the Dingle peninsula, passing many ruined beehive huts which did not look as if they were going to yield up any old secrets at all. That would be the famous Gallarus Oratory there, which I did not even bother to stop to look around, and mostly it was a case of winding lanes, stray donkeys and those smart new bungalows. You have to travel a long way in Ireland to come across an old bothy with a turf roof now.

Yes, this was the morning when I was clearly going to

1

have to think about getting a proper job. I would never find anything in Ireland but rain, still less come even close to working out what it means to be a Celt here. This was the day in which I was finally going to be undone and, to make matters far worse, I recollected that I had long received – and spent – the advance for this book. Authors will say anything when they are trying to winkle an advance out of a publisher and here, large as life and twice as nasty, was my comeuppance. My headache thickened a good four degrees and, for a moment, I thought my nose was going to start bleeding with fear.

But then a small Irish miracle came to my rescue: the rain stopped and what looked very much like the sun broke through the clouds. I parked on the quay in Dingle harbour and had this definite feeling in my nose that matters were going to improve quickly. This raggle-taggle village had a real sense of fun about it and there were lots of fishing boats moored all along the quay decked out in many flags advertising such as Harp, Budweiser, Murphy's and Guinness.

There was some sort of carnival in the offing and as I nosed around a bit more I discovered that, in a sense, Dingle was permanently locked in one long carnival; one sorry statistic virtually tells the whole story: Dingle, with a population of 1500, has forty-five pubs. There is roughly one pub for every thirty people and, oh boy, what pubs they turned out to be. A few are chintzy tourist bars with tasselled curtains and gaudy coloured lights, but most are nicotine-stained, wood-panelled shebeens with gloomy corners and sawdust on the floorboards, populated by old scoundrels in flat caps perched above their pints of Guinness and ready to tell some highly improbable tale at the touch of an invisible button. Many talk in a totally incomprehensible gibberish, from which meaning emerges only fitfully, while many more give forth endless and varying unsolicited opinions on everything to do with philosophy, politics, religion and even who

2

should be picked and who should be dropped from the Welsh – yes, Welsh – rugby team. This gale of complex and contradictory opinion is also leavened by lots of cigarette smoke and a more or less continual stream of bad language. Your average Dingle pub will be full of inveterate liars, wild analysis, squalling babies and an endless peppering of four-letter words, as I soon found out. They will even jam the four-lettered word into the middle of long words too.

After almost three years of being teetotal I stood at the bar of the first pub I walked into for about five minutes, with three men talking to me at the same time, and decided there and then that teetotalism was wholly inappropriate in Dingle. I ordered my first glass in three years and drank it down in a trice before ordering another. Quite soon I felt I had practically grown up in that bar and had a sharp and lasting insight into Irish alcoholism. Here you drink because that is what everyone else does. You drink because you want to belong to the tribe and not left out in the street on your own. When I asked what time the bar closed the barman waved his hand, squinted a bit in thought and said: 'Oh sometime in late September.'

The lubricant of all this wild talk was 'the black stuff' on which half of Ireland may have been reared if not actually conceived. Almost all the men I met in Dingle seemed not to eat anything at all, managing on a dozen or so pints of Guinness a day. One claimed that his gravestone was going to be constructed entirely of empty Guinness bottles. Poured with elaborate care the drink has a thick head of creamy foam atop a long black body with white tidal movements still swirling around inside it. The bouquet has the faint aroma of old socks until you take the first sip which always gives you a nice white moustache you either lick off or wipe away with the sleeve of your jacket. You then work your way down the glass, foaming ringlet by foaming ringlet. A night on the black stuff is a little like eating a dozen Mars bars and it finally gives you the sleep of the dead. The men often claim that it adds to their sexual prowess even if the women know otherwise. It certainly makes them fart like ducks.

But the truly odd feature of many of these bars was that they doubled up as shops. Thus you could get a drink at one counter and buy a book on the other side. There are pubs here which are butcher shops and a grocery shop where the locals can sit for an evening and get totally bladdered as they buy all their groceries before loading them on their handlebars and then cycling home sideways. One pub in Kilkenny, I was told, had a garden centre out the front with a bar inside and a room out the back for selling guns and another for coffins. Now that's what I call hedging your business bets.

One of my favourite bars in Dingle was Dick Mack's, a shoe shop where you could get your shoes tapped at one counter while you drink at the other. Wellingtons and bovver boots hung in clumps overhead as tall story followed tall story. 'There was this dog in here the other week, couldn't hold his beer at all he couldn't. Drank so much Guinness one night he cocked his leg to have a wee and fell flat on his back.'

The stories became even wilder in Mrs Griffin's bar down on the quay. Mrs Griffin had clearly worked hard to keep this bar in the same state of dilapidation for the last forty years. It was entirely devoid of any kind of ornament or indeed almost anything to do with the twentieth century. When I asked for the lavatory she said that it was 'out the back and up against the wall'. They once had a canary in the bar but it died of the drink, she recalled with a faint tear in her eye. 'We always put whiskey in its milk for Christmas and it would warble a song and then fall off its perch. Cirrhosis of the liver got it in the end. Poor t'ing sang beautiful when it was sober an' all.'

The next morning most of the town turned out for the eleven o'clock Mass and the church was packed. The

4

priest spoke well but I then noticed another curious feature of Irish spiritual life: there were quite a few elderly men standing inside the vestry doors, a few visibly twitching with hangovers, unwilling to actually step inside the church but not quite capable of rejecting the whole business either. So they hung around the doors, neither in nor out, and when the Mass was over these holy ditherers immediately made their way back to the pubs and another day on the Mars bars.

The priest then led a procession with a fife and drum band down to the quay where we were about to take part in Dingle's annual Blessing of the Boats. The priest took a lifeboat out into the middle of the bay where he parked and, afterwards, we packed into some sixty fishing boats and sailed out in his wake; as we sailed round him he duly blessed us all. Every deck of every ship was jammed with little heads as the whole town and its dog received the Blessing. Behind us was a ghost village. 'A good time for criminals to start a crime wave,' I mused aloud, but the man next to me said that there was no crime in Dingle. Ah well not yet.

As the flotilla continued sailing, Fungie, the famous Dingle dolphin, came out to meet the boats, leaping from one to the other in fantastic supercharged arcs. Fungie is on a long-term contract with the Irish Tourist Board and people come from all over the world to swim with him – provided he is in a playful mood.

We also, in our larger boat, nearly managed the historic feat of running down Charlie Haughey, the former Taosieach of Ireland, in his smaller boat. I had last seen Charlie some twenty-five years earlier in a Dublin dock, when I was a reporter for *The Sunday Times* and he had been up on a gun-running charge which he got off. And here he was again, not looking a day older, in his denim skipper's cap and acting the part of Captain Birds Eye as he kept bossing everyone around as usual. He now lives on one of the nearby Blasket Islands which he also owns.

I had been in Dingle for more than twenty-four hours and had not eaten so much as a packet of crisps, which was just as well since that night I had – for £12 – one of the biggest and best meals of my life. It was the traditional barbecue for the Blessing of the Boats in the garden of Bennard's Hotel and the word in Dick Mack's was that you had to get there early before everyone else polished off the lot. I duly got there early along with everyone else and began with six oysters, a couple of spare ribs, a lump of rice, a splodge of stew, some barbecue sauce and a fat steak. 'Are you wanting one or two now?' And this was but the first course since I then had six crab claws, some monkfish, a couple of herrings and, if there had been any room left, which there was not, some ice cream and a chocolate cake. Pfui! My packed belly did not have the room to sort out so much as a small belch and I merely sat like some bloated Buddha at a table in the corner of the dance marquee, staring into space and unable to speak.

Captain Birds Eye then handed out silver cups to the skippers of the best dressed boats and soon the whole crowd, full of hiccups and happiness, was dancing to the jigs and reels of a local band. These jigs are more infectious than measles; even after so much to eat, I had begun dancing with a laughing, black-eyed woman when I was most disconcerted to find a huge, gnarled hand on my shoulder. 'You be careful now,' a voice rasped. 'You're dancing with my mother.'

Yet it was only some time after I had driven my hangover out of Dingle that I began to understand that I had, in fact, made something of a start on my personal investigation into the nature of the Celt.

For surely what I had found in those lively bars was the famous crack, that pure and abiding quality of Irishness which had been going for thousands of years. By this I mean the way in which they can be devastatingly frank in the face of what they perceive as weakness or softness; the

6

way that, just like the ancient poets, their lips can become aflame with scorching sarcasm towards someone who arouses their ire; the way they can dismantle whole theological systems with a string of cuss words; and how they fully understand and already know all the secrets that the Government will not tell them.

This gift for endless blarney has clearly kept flowing like the mightiest river. Not surprisingly, Blarney Castle – with its stone which is said to bestow eternal eloquence on anyone who kisses it – was not too many miles away.

And then there was the drink, the music and the dancing. These too would surely find a prime place in any investigation into the nature of a Celt and I was sure I was going to come across a lot more of them before my inquiries were through. The Blessing of the Boats too would have a peculiarly Celtic flavour in so far as everything was blessed in the Middle Ages. The early Celts had a blessing for everything.

Such discoveries were hardly going to qualify me for a doctorate on the Celts but they were, at least, a start.

The afternoon was awash with thin, brittle sunshine and I stopped on the edge of a bog and walked down to the area where the men had been cutting the turves, picking one up in my hands. It was surprisingly heavy and dry, immediately breaking up in my clumsy grip and falling on my shoes in a noisy shower. Its smell was rich and slightly acrid and its taste was not much to write home about either.

It was difficult to believe this lump of earth had always been the basic unit of energy in Ireland. Such turves had always kept the Irish warm; without such crumbling lumps they would all have frozen solid centuries ago.

In front of me was a still, black pond with several dead lilies floating pointlessly on its surface. Midges swarmed in small, busy clouds nearby and, further out again, was the vast natural wilderness of Connemara with distant, purple mountains patched unevenly with sunshine and shadow. But all around me was bog and yet more bog, dotted with small black pools and vivid with the natural colours of a Connemara autumn. The grass and moss had turned a dark brown and the bracken was mauve even if the yellow gorse seemed, if anything, to be getting brighter. This land turns to its most fiery and splendid, however, when a huge orb of sunshine gets trapped between those two distant mountains, turning everything into luminous rhapsody and making even that ruined croft look as new and welcoming as on the day it was built. Yet it is the silence out here that gets right inside you and I was sure you could haunt these bogs for centuries and still hear nothing louder than the blood moving around inside your ears.

It would be a brave or desperate man who would want to eke out a living on this rock-strewn land. This is the poorest area of the poorest region of the poorest country in the European Union. Even Connemara ponies, renowned for their toughness, find it hard poking around here looking for something more appetizing than rocks to eat. Skinny sheep often take shelter behind high stone walls. Little pyramids of hay can be seen sitting around with small tarpaulins tied to the tops of their heads.

But 'tis an ill wind . . . the otters are doing well out this way and only that morning I had seen one fishing in the river in the middle of Galway city. I was walking over a bridge towards the cathedral when I spotted this thing in the river. More and more of us gathered to watch it. 'Ah it looks like a dog but its ears are too small,' said one.

The otter came up and looked around for a bit, revealing its white chin and huge black eyes before diving again. You could follow its path by the long rippling Vs on the water. At one stage a seagull began circling it noisily when it came up with a big fish in its mouth. But the otter was not about to share its fish with anyone – still less that noisy gull – and, after shaking the fish around for a while, as if softening it up, duly swallowed the lot.

Galway, the gateway to Connemara, is a fine city and every corner seemed to have some stone animal or angel staring back at you. The pricy shops and cafés are full of fun too, with lots of larky pubs amok with the sound of fiddles, and, on the streets themselves, there were any number of buskers entertaining a passing procession of short arms and deep pockets.

I sniffed at my crumbling lump of turf again. All the nameless and long terrors of Irish history seem to have grown out of her earth and, as you travel around these parts, you can occasionally spot the outlines of the dead 'lazybeds' of that potato crop which kept failing so disastrously in the mid-nineteenth century. The ghosts of those who starved still haunt these parts, they say, and on very quiet nights when nothing moves in the moonlight, you can still spot these terrible figures, black-eyed and green-mouthed from eating grass, stumbling down the road to Galway in the often forlorn hope of a 'coffin' ship to America and a full belly.

These stories remain as harrowing as the land that gave them birth and, looking out on those evil, black ponds, I wondered how even otters have managed to survive. Only the graveyards did well around these parts and they are here still, full of wonky stone Celtic crosses and unkempt grassy mounds.

But there have been wonderful and miraculous events around here too. St Patrick once climbed that mountain over there and chanted a prayer a thousand times for the soul of all Ireland. St Colman came here from Lindisfarne to set up his stall in that village down the way and, much, much later, John Alcock and Arthur Browne dropped out of the Connemara sky into that bog there, the first to fly the Atlantic, in June 1919.

Yet, just standing here holding a breaking turf and looking out towards those distant mountains, with this Connemara silence swirling around me, I really did feel that I could start making some intelligent guesses at the nature of the Celtic faith here.

This, surely, was the faith of ancestral memory, brought to long fruition by much suffering. This was a faith that was essentially simple and grew out of the land which yielded so little of itself. It was a faith that grew out of a human need for more than had been given. It was a faith that owed much to the grandeur of nature and encouraged a direct, personal relationship with God.

I was sure that I was going to work out a lot more about the nature of this faith and its relationship with the natural world and, with the sun taking up its final glorious position between those two mountains, I carefully put back my broken turf on the pile, fearful that perhaps some angry bog man might return and demand that I pay for the lot.

There is a growling melancholy about the Aran Islands which you pick up on almost as soon as you approach them on the ferry. You can see this bleak sadness in the raddled weather-beaten crosses in the cemetery; it is also in the high ragged stone walls which keep criss-crossing the island; in the ruined hill-forts and the rusty wreck of that freighter sitting perilously on the rocks of the foreshore. But most of all it is in the sheer emptiness of the islands, since no one seems to be moving anywhere. A plague may well have wiped out everyone only yesterday and I half expected some tumbleweed to start rolling down between the scattered houses at any moment.

I was the only person to land on Inisheer, the smallest of the Arans, that afternoon and I wandered up the rising lanes and through the houses looking for a B. & B. I knocked on a few doors and no one answered. All that could be heard were the winds howling softly through holes in the stone walls. Vast lanterns of light hung in the air around my head.

Down below, upturned fishing currachs lay on the beach. Lobster pots sat piled up on the quay and a few of the houses had turf roofs even if they were clearly derelict. My nose did occasionally pick up the smell of the burning sod; a sickly smell, I have always thought, good for killing mice or at least driving them out. I had an Irish friend who liked to burn turves at her London parties and it sometimes got so bad we had to take our drinks and stand out in the street.

But, my oh my, this was a lonely and barren place. It was not too many years ago, I had been told, that the islanders had to break up the limestone with sledgehammers to find sufficient soil for their crops and everything was fertilized by seaweed which had to be brought up from the sea by donkey and cart.

Yet on my way back down to the quay to see if there was a room in the hotel I noticed that there were, in fact, plenty of eyes watching me, since almost every house seemed to have a dog in the garden who – unlike their yapping, snarling brethren on the mainland – were entirely friendly. A few wandered out to sniff my ankles or roll on their backs in the forlorn hope of having their bellies tickled.

Down at the hotel it again looked like the set of *Death in Venice* with everyone packed up and fled from some mysterious plague. I was even told to find my own room and that they never really bothered with keys. Many guests had gone only that morning, I learned, after being stranded here for three days. The weather makes it difficult to operate a regular ferry service. It might go tomorrow but there again it might not. Aran islanders rarely give a straight answer to a straight question – particularly if the question is something to do with ferry times. A Spaniard had been there the other week and they had asked him to

11

explain the concept of *mañana*; when he did, they said they had nothing on the Arans to express quite that sense of urgency.

I went out later wandering along the twisting stone lanes when I met a man digging up fat potatoes with his hands. I helped him pick enough for his kids' tea. Dara Ó Conaola was his name, he said, and he was a writer. He was born in the middle island of Inishmaan and trained as a woodwork teacher in Galway. In the sixties he was involved in civil rights – 'I did my bit protesting and marching' – and finally began a successful campaign to set up a school here in Inisheer where he returned with his wife and kids. You could tell he had once been a good agitator, with his long, curly hair, a wild rebellious glint in his eye, and a certain bouncing mien that would have looked about right on the barricades.

He has written seven books and he gave me his latest, *Night Ructions*, which is a wonderful book, thick with the spirit of the island. In its pages he spells out what I had been sniffing around all day; the loneliness and yet intense intimacy of the place. He brings it all to life, as the old but useful cliché has it, from the big slob of a spider about to crashland on the cupboard to the eventide, when the dung beetle was going behind the dock leaf, or the dog who was lying in a sunbeam, or the way the island was being engulfed with the cold venom of spring. His sentences are as spare as the bleak Aran stones.

Dara grew up listening to his father's stories on the hearth and inherited the secret of the *seanchai*, bestowed on the traditional story-teller. Like his rather more famous fellow Aran islander, Liam O'Flaherty, he writes with a tingling sense of narrative which effortlessly captures even the most wandering concentration, and you can all but hear the fury of storms on winter nights in his words. Every paragraph seems to be embroidered with the sound effects of the chimney or the whistling kettle. The hearth has always been the sacred centre of learning for all us Celts; everything that was truly valuable was learned on the hearth.

His art grew out of family tradition since his family has been telling stories for hundreds of years, and he often writes about his own family house built in 1839. His great-grandfather was about to build it on another part of the island when a travelling man warned him that a fairy palace was once there and they'd never leave him in peace. And they didn't either.

Later I was passing the zig-zag line of yet more stone walls when I came across a man deep in conversation with his donkey. 'Ah it's an amazing place to live,' he told me when he finished his chat. 'You dig what you need and what with a cow or two life is powerful easy it is. Me and the donkey here are all we need. We'll be buried together. But youngsters don't want to know all about that now. If they can't get a tractor or press a button for anything they need they don't want to know.'

What I found intriguing about the old boys I spoke to was that there was no complaint with them – unlike Welsh farmers who are often full of nothing else. If anyone found a way of packaging this Aran contentment he would indeed make a fortune and I could picture this man and his donkey buried together out in that cemetery for all eternity, his arms around the donkey's neck as they both lay listening to those bleak sounds of the sea and the whistling winds.

I was standing quietly on the prow of the next hill, gazing out over the hummocky island when the faint shiver of a far-off memory passed through my mind. Then this shiver hardened and I found myself walking down the hill with a leather satchel full of books and a water bottle around my shoulders, holding a staff and wearing only a threadbare cassock of grey Aran wool. I was going to say goodbye.

Tiny sandstorms were sweeping along the stone walls as I walked into a large compound with two dozen circular huts scattered around a huge lecture hall. The walls of the huts were made of wicker and the lecture hall was a rough stone washed with lime. Over to one side of the compound was a high Celtic stone cross and a goatskin was pegged out on a wooden frame, drying in the wind. Hungry chickens were foraging almost everywhere.

I hung around outside the lecture hall indecisively. Inside Enda was giving one of his rather more abstruse lectures in Latin to about thirty students on wooden benches. Others, in their own dark huts, were studying Scripture or reciting psalms aloud in the thin, smokey light given off by the tallow candles. They too were wearing grey Aran cassocks and many of them had lately taken to wearing make-up, for some strange reason.

This had been my home for so long now I simply did not want to leave it; this polished scholastic air had become my air and I so wanted to breathe it for the rest of my days. Strange emotions clogged up my throat and I was afraid that I was going to cry.

Enda was showing no sign of finishing his lecture so I went over to the scriptorium and hung around outside for a while. It was in there that I had first learned to write business letters and how to register property, and how to make calculations by which we arrived at such important dates as Easter. We worked long into every night using goose or crow feathers as quills; yes, we learned all the tricks in there from using knives and needles to cut into the vellum and even importing some of our colours like lapus lazuli from Afghanistan.

Enda finished his lecture and came out to see me, as he had promised, putting his arm around my shoulders as we walked back up that hill together. He told me there

14

would always be a home for me here but it was now time to take my learning and teaching out into Erin. 'This is what God is asking of you,' he continued. 'But in the end it just comes down to belief and trust. All you have to do is believe in the truth and trust in the nature of God's grace. Then your career is bound to be a success.'

But I was not convinced, still worried, in fact, that I had been kicked out because I had kept giving away our corn to the Aran poor. I had always been a bit of a rebel and now they were getting rid of me.

When I bade Enda farewell with a holy kiss I was still anxious and worried about everything as I walked down to the quay where my boat was waiting. I stopped still, hearing the flapping of a huge pair of wings deep within the Aran light, the usual sign of the presence of a ministering angel.

A huge tree began forming in the very air in front of me, with many birds swooping down out of the sky to feed on the bunches of fruit dangling off the many strong branches. You, Ciaran, are going to be the tree of all Ireland, the vision told me. You are going to become as strong as this trunk and the Irish people are going to feed off your teachings in the same way as all these birds are feeding off your fruit. They are going to come to you for shelter from all the storms of evil which will sweep the land and, when you finally die, your body will be recycled into the earth, nourishing the roots of other trees who will also, in their turn, offer food and shelter to the people.

So go out, my dear Ciaran, and build a church on Shannon's banks.

2

Lost in Snowdonia

THE BARE MOUNTAIN has always been a central feature in the Celtic landscape; it has always been a holy place, both near to heaven and far from the madding throng; a place set apart for praise, visions and commandments. And so it was that I tried to get a foothold on the Celtic Heart on the majestic mountain range of Snowdonia, traditionally home to all the old Welsh gods.

But this proved to be a truly difficult task because, despite their glamorous and highly spiritual image, I actually hate mountains, which are often sullen, dull piles of rock, unwilling to part with their secrets and frequently taking an almost perverse delight in either exhausting you or else tumbling you down their rubbled slopes, whereupon you can end up with a broken leg or even dead with a broken neck. Also, to be perfectly honest, it would not exactly ruin my day if all mountains were flattened, so it was with not too much pleasure that I set out of Llanberis early one winter morning to climb Snowdon.

I drove up the foothills as far as I could, parking next to a ruined farm before setting out on foot. Every inch of the way was pure misery as almost every other walker in Wales went striding past me at close on a hundred miles an hour. These walkers looked like they knew what they were doing, with their backpacks, climbing boots and legs packed with Weetabix muscles. My misery thickened considerably when it began to drizzle with cold rain and nowhere is rain drizzlier or colder than up here on

16

Snowdon. White sheep with stupid eyes watched me before jerking away and soon I was so miserable I did not even stop to admire the rocky views.

Well I was going to find out nothing useful to my research carrying on like this and, after another half hour of damp misery, I gave up my assault on the mountain. I returned to my camper van only to find it blocked in the lane by a farmer's Land Rover; this led to a fantastic and heated argument before he finally agreed to move it so that I could get out. It was all to do with teaching people like me a lesson, the miserable old drone kept droning on, as if I went there every morning at the crack of dawn and parked right in that spot with acres of mountain all around, purely and deliberately to stop him getting out onto the slopes to count his sheep.

I had not completely given up on the mountain angle so the next day I got in touch with the Royal Air Force based in Valley in Anglesey and managed to catch a ride on one of their Wessex helicopters which they use to train their pilots over Snowdonia. Now that they have no war to fight and *Jim'll Fix It* has stopped running on television they still take their public relations seriously even if they did make it clear that they were not keen to have me on board, making me promise to keep my mouth shut for the duration of the flight and indeed not to try to talk about anything at all while they got on with their training. They had not long ago lost one of their Wessexs in a nearby lake and they were not keen on doing that again.

And so it turned out that, instead of stumbling painfully up a mountain in the rain, I was now actually flying dumbly over one, happier and more thrilled than any old scribbler had a right to be, helmeted and dressed up like Tom Cruise in *Top Gun*, with the side door of the helicopter open and icy winds blasting in from every direction. The dark purple tips of the mountain peaks poked up from beneath snowy hazes and the sky was the clearest and most ravishing blue. Those parts of the

17

mountains that were basking in the sun were brown and gold and those that were not were white and icy. Lone climbers waved at us as we turned and turned again with the helicopter's shadow moving across the crags and slopes like a giant space-age dragonfly.

Winds are the great problem when flying helicopters in the mountains and we kept dropping flares to work out the direction of the wind which, in some parts, can start blowing like a small tempest. Out here the weather can also change dramatically within minutes, which is why so many climbers often get into trouble on the slopes and have to be winched to safety by helicopter. But no such problems on this virtually windless morning as we banked up to the summit dropping coloured flares behind us and just hung there, right on top of the roof of Wales, with views of hundreds of miles in every direction.

A long ridge ran directly away from the peak itself with our yellow and red smoke flares billowing up from various places as if a few gangs of Red Indians were having a good chat over their morning coffee. Deep in the crevices there were hidden pools and secretive streams but, as always, it was the sheer strength and durability of the mountains that impressed you. The Red Indians always used to say that only the stones live for ever.

Yes, it was simply amazing hovering up there, but the trouble was this was almost no use at all to my research since, slippery though my arguments might get and highly tenuous though the links might be, I just could not see how I was going to work RAF smoke flares, Snowdon's wind patterns and the language of Red Indians into a meditation on the Celtic Heart.

But I *still* did not give up on the mountain angle since, a few days later, I remembered that there was, in fact, a nicer and more accessible mountain in the Snowdonia range called Cadair Idris. This really was a sacred peak of high drama and shimmering visions so beloved of the

18

essentially visionary and dramatic Celtic Heart. Mary Jones, a young peasant girl, had walked over this peak barefoot in 1800 to call on Thomas Charles in Bala asking if he would sell her a Bible. Charles was so inspired by her long walk that he later set up the British and Foreign Bible Society. The evangelist George Fox was also vouchsafed a vision up there, and here too Thomas Love Peacock reflected 'with astonishment and pity on the madness of the multitude'. Legend has it that, if you spend the night on Idris's chair at the peak, you will either go barmy or be endowed with wondrous poetical powers. Or both.

Yes, I was bound to get hundreds, if not thousands of barmy, poetical words out of this expedition, so I duly spent the night in my van in a field dotted with sheep dung next to a stream before making myself several cups of coffee early the next morning and hurling myself on said slope, with a Mars bar in one pocket and a can of Coke in the other, determined to claim the peak for the Queen. THE CHAIR OF IDRIS IS YOURS YOUR MAJESTY, the telegram would run.

The first part of the climb, through a wood and next to a waterfall, was easy enough, except that I lost the path and ended up scrambling over some mossy rocks and up through a small waterfall. This was exquisitely difficult and, at one point, I was on all fours clinging to the rocks, with freezing water flowing through my fingers and filling up my boots, like some petrified salmon which had not only forgotten how to leap but had lost its sense of direction.

I continued scrambling on up that waterfall for almost an hour and those parts of me that were not soaked through were sweating profusely. At last I came upon a decent clearing in the woodland to sit down and rest, only to find the exploded carcass of a sheep right there with hanks of white wool scattered around and its skeleton clearly picked clean by the crows. Its head was still strangely intact – perhaps crows simply do not like sheep's head – with its eyes staring at me balefully. I went for a walk up here and, oh brother, look what happened to me, those eyes said. I once walked proud on the mountain and look how I ended up.

It was the pure stench of that carcass that drove me on when the climb became almost vertical and I was reasonably sure I was going to end up in much the same state as that dead sheep. I was also clearly lost and I wondered if those boys in RAF Valley would find me in one of their Wessexs before the crows also picked *my* body clean. Would the crows leave my eyes alone too, I wanted to know. Or would they pick the whole of my head clean? Or start at my toes perhaps and work their way up? Or chip away at my teeth and loosen all my fillings? Perhaps I was going barmy sooner than might be expected? And I certainly could not detect any stirrings of any wondrous poetical powers in my imagination.

I hauled myself up on my elbows onto the next rocky plateau and came nose to nose with yet another sheep's dead body and, oh mummy, there was another corpse nearby which did not even have a head. Their stink was industrial and the inevitable question was: if these sheep couldn't survive up here, what chance did I have? To make matters worse it began to snow lightly and I knew then I'd had it for sure. I just knew that it was going to be a royal flush of frostbite, hypothermia and double pneumonia.

But, with my demise imminent, I somehow managed to scramble out onto the mountain summit where the grass was a mysterious dark black. But nevertheless I'd done it; I'd done it. This had been a triumph of human perseverance; a day when the human spirit had taken on one of the last great physical challenges and won all. My fear and pain drained straight out of my wet boots and I did a little jig of joy around and around the black grass.

A huge wind was roaring up out of a nearby valley and I leaned into it with my arms windmilling, smiling at the immensity of my achievement. Cold snowflakes dissolved warmly in my eyes and I actually seemed to be hang-gliding on the warmth of my own success. Sherpa Davies had prevailed against the most bitter elements by struggling up the snowbound slopes of death, through icy rivers and sheep graveyards, to conquer the great peak of Cadair Idris. THE CHAIR OF IDRIS IS YOURS YOUR MAJESTY. Next stop Everest and no messing about. I sat down for a celebratory Mars bar and a loyal toast of Coke.

But within minutes I realized something had gone badly wrong. A huge body of mist went striding past and I saw that I was in fact on the next peak to a surprisingly high mountain. Lumps of chocolate fell out of my mouth as celebration turned to despair. That was Cadair Idris. This was another mountain altogether. The sorry truth was I had been labouring heroically all morning to get up the wrong mountain.

So it was a dejected Sherpa Davies who crossed a wide ravine, with the sheep taking a break from their munching to nudge one another and laugh out loud, as he scrambled to get down there and over onto the right mountain. And it was a very fagged-out Sherpa Davies, with legs like a couple of wobbling jellyfish, who kicked his way disconsolately through the bracken before coming to the small lake of Llyn Cau, about half way up, knowing that he was not about to claim the summit for the Queen or Prince Charles or indeed anyone else that morning.

I was so fed up I was not even worried about the snow any more; it could turn into a blizzard or even an avalanche for all I cared. A bank of mist started tracking me downwards and, for a while, it seemed that I was trudging down a sort of ghostly elevator. Further on yet another waterfall was bursting out of the high grey and black slopes and I sat down on a rock where, after experiencing a wide variety of emotions ranging from failure to failure, I decided I was not only going to give up on the mountain angle in my future research but, with any luck, give up on mountains altogether *for the rest of my days.*

More mists kept swirling around me and gaps opened up in them, offering enthralling glimpses of the mountains and valleys. The silence of the morning was total when I felt what I can only describe as a complete falling away. Everything in my mind – the voices, the images, the memories and the million other things that keep wandering through it – were all cleared out and I was left with what the philosopher Locke called a *tabula rasa.* Then, with all that silence penetrating right inside me, my actual body seemed to lift off into the very air too and I became pure spirit, floating there above a huge valley, warmly and steadily, like one of those Wessexs.

It was not a vision in any sense, since I have seen visions which contained such terror and violence that I fervently hope I never see another. This was a trance-like state of being in which I felt transported directly into the Kingdom of God; a moment when I just knew that, even in times of difficulty and failure, we were always being watched over and that, even in the oddest and lowest situations, there is indeed meaning in everything.

And this, I also later saw, was something to do with what I had been looking for, since I was not interested in the complex history of the Celts nor the wide variety of countries from which they had hailed, nor indeed their bizarre folktales or unlikely mythology, so much as how they felt and how they came to believe in what they believed and what touched them deep down.

So up here perhaps I had finally learned something about their preparedness to believe in the invisible; their ability to be moved and shaped and even educated by, well, nothing at all but space and light and the way odd snowflakes drift down misty valley walls.

Later that afternoon I was sitting on the back step of my van eating an orange with great gouts of juice running over my fingers and down my chin when I had an absolutely brilliant idea. I am not at all sure where brilliant ideas come from – particularly when you are more concerned with eating an orange – but one moment there is nothing but blankness up top and the next there is this idea just sitting there like some strange and gaudy budgie which has materialized out of nowhere.

If I really wanted to find out more about the Celtic Heart then why didn't I go over to Llŷn and interview that great Celt himself, the poet priest R. S. Thomas? Who knew more about the tortured soul of the Welsh than this old Celtic magician who had once described Wales as 'a land of romance and danger, a secret land' or, rather more memorably, as 'the bright hill under the black cloud'.

For some, old R. S. was one of the three leading religious poets of the twentieth century; a man whose work had set out to find the God of the interstices; a poet/priest who had so chillingly and exactly tried to define what it was to be a Celt on his knees at prayer before an altar in an old stone chapel. This was the one man who really knew all about the vagaries of the Celtic Heart. Yes. Absolutely brilliant. A bit of poetic gravitas. Just what I needed at this point.

The trouble was I had long had a spiky relationship with old R. S. and was not exactly top of his Christmas card list. Some years back *The Times* had asked me to write a profile of him, so I duly wrote him a letter, full of sly flattery and obsequious homage. I also enclosed a religious book I had written which had won an award, hoping it would impress him. Well it did not, since a few weeks later I received a postcard thanking me for the book but adding that he had no wish to be profiled in *The Times* and he would be grateful if I told them so.

His rudeness to visitors has long been a Celtic legend in its own right. An American student once travelled to Wales, knocked on his door to pay tribute and, after he had explained how he had been a lifelong fan and that old R. S.'s poetry had changed his life, the door was slammed in his face. An Arts Council director drove the length of Wales to present him with a cheque which R. S. did indeed accept, only to then slam the door in his face too.

I was pretty broke when *The Times* asked me to profile him and, as they were then paying up to £1,000 for a profile, I decided to risk a flattened nose and knocked on his cottage door in the grounds of Plas Y Rhiw manor near Aberdaron. The old dragon finally appeared and, with his lower lip quivering in anger, barked 'Yes?'

I explained who I was and he immediately asked me if I was working for *The Times*. Well yes and no, Mr Thomas. A bit. What do you mean a bit? You're not working for *The Western Mail* are you? *The Western Mail* had also long been another pretty rampant bee in old R. S.'s bonnet. Well not really, Mr Thomas. But now and then. I'm trying to write something about the history of the area, I blustered on, getting all vague, and if you could give me ten minutes that would be really, really helpful. About the history of the Llŷn. That's all. Nothing too difficult or, er, controversial.

'I don't speak to the English media and it's not *the* Llŷn, it's Llŷn. You English are always getting it wrong.'

I held up my hands suitably chastised. I was as Welsh as he was but wasn't about to start an argument on the subject. All I wanted to do was get in through that door and I would even have kissed his boots if it would have advanced my cause. But then, with him still staring down at me as if I wanted to cut off his electricity, he, to my complete amazement, invited me in saying that I could have ten minutes. And no more. On the history of the area. And nothing else.

I could not believe I had actually got into the old poet's lair, where so many others had failed before me, but there he was leading me into his back room with its books and bare floorboards. He even told me to watch that I didn't bump my head on the doorway *and* pulled out a chair for me to sit down on. Well, well Mr Thomas, this is all very nice isn't it? Disappointingly there was no sign of a television or newspapers though I did spot a portable radio. I just loved the notion of Mr Thomas pulling on his slippers and sitting down in the evening, getting ready to watch *EastEnders*.

He began our chat by complaining that he had always been misquoted as when it was said that he had been urging the Welsh to daub slogans on – or set fire to – English homes in Wales. But the English media were all the same weren't they? They were only interested in sensationalism and he tried not to take much notice but it was difficult at times. 'I still write about what it's like in this area, the tensions between the old life and the way it's being threatened by contemporary life, media exploitation and second homes. The trouble is that I still have to use English for my poetry; I can't seem to write poetry in Welsh, but I have been writing some prayers in Welsh.'

He had been retired for fourteen years but had just started conducting services in the local church otherwise it would have closed. 'But hold on.' One of his very long forefingers rose up and pointed at me. 'What's all this got to do with the history of Llŷn?'

His hands were simply enormous with long, concert pianist's fingers; a cliff face of a forehead and a tight, down-turned mouth which, you just knew, had known long hours of quiet despair as he wrestled with his notions such as the *deus absconditus*, the God who is

25

there by not being there and the 'untenanted cross'. But it was good to hear his reputation for rudeness was not exactly unfounded because, when I mentioned my book which I had sent him, he immediately denounced it as 'Anglicanized media rubbish' whatever that might be. 'Well it did win an award Mr Thomas,' I pointed out, pained.

'Oh they give awards to anything at all these days,' he snorted.

If he was so opposed to the Anglicanized media, I asked him, why then had he agreed to appear on television's *South Bank Show* recently, particularly as he had clearly wanted nothing to do with *The Times*? Hah, he said, they had offered him thousands of pounds and he wasn't a wealthy man. Oh, so he will talk to the hated Anglican media for thousands of pounds then? Bit of a contradiction here isn't there?

'Oh I know there's a lot of contradictions in my position but it's just the way I am.'

I was never quite sure if he had read the profile I had written about him, which finally came out in *The Western Mail* and not *The Times*, and was not entirely friendly, accusing him of pinheaded tribalism. So it was with not too much confidence that I drove over to his home to chance my arm again on his front door.

Llŷn is a thick fist of land which pokes out of the north-west corner of Wales; the Land's End of Wales, some call it, just sixteen miles long and up to ten miles wide, which, by reason of its isolation, may be one of the last bastions of Welshness. A sprinkling of Welsh monoglots still live in Llŷn and that most musical of languages is used in almost all day-to-day life. Every village has its own chapel with elders walking there on Sundays with fat Bibles under their arms, and almost everywhere you turn the land is dotted with ancient burial grounds, strange henges and stone axe factories. The roar of the waves is never far away and this is a pilgrimage route to Bardsey Island or Ynys Enlli, the sacred island of the saints which lies amidst treacherous currents just off the peninsula tip.

The poet's home is a whitewashed cottage standing high on a headland and looking out over the sea where a constant procession of breakers keep coming in high and proud before bashing their brains out on the rocks. Seagulls circled and dived around the cottage as I approached and I really did feel nervous about trying to beard the old dragon in his lair again; but there was just a chance that he might be in a generous and magnanimous mood towards uninvited visitors, since he had recently been nominated for the Nobel prize for literature, although, as it later turned out, unsuccessfully.

Yet it was, I have to admit, with a great deal of relief that I discovered that, in fact, the old dragon had long fled his lair and I would learn nothing about his thoughts about the Celts, or indeed anything else, since the cottage was empty and the rooms deserted. Further inquiries revealed that he had long got fed up with visitors – particularly ones from the media – so had gone to live in nearby Anglesey where he hoped he would get some peace and quiet.

And who, in their right mind, could blame him for that?

3

A Keening in Dunblane

—⊷—

IT WAS A GREY, thin, drizzling dawn as a group of us stood on a low shoreline, surrounded by an even lower loch and all of us silent for a while with a sense of standing somewhere before the start of history. Nothing seemed to have been touched or a single stone ever moved throughout these flat islands of creeping mists where rainbows started to build briefly in pockets of sunshine only to disappear again through yet more misty doorways.

A small group of us from Wales had come to the Orkneys, searching for our spiritual roots and, normally a chattering bunch with lots of seagull laughter, we were quiet now as we peered around this terrible, bleak place, full of rogue winds and weeping skies where, a man in Kirkwall had told me, they have three months of rain a year and then nine months of bad weather.

The journey here had been a singular one too; a lively bounce from one wave to the next on the ferry out of Scrabster to the islands themselves, and then a drive along lots of causeways built with huge concrete blocks and surrounding the smooth waters of Scapa Flow. Here the hulls of the scuttled German navy still lie on their sides, many visible yet all rusty now, doubtless dreaming drowned dreams of their old glory days when they belched black smoke and fired lots of big guns. A patch of stray sunshine marked the spot where a U-boat had once slunk into these waters and sunk the battleship Ark Royal, with the loss of more than 200 lives.

But apart from these wrecks, this area just has to be as it was on the first day of creation. With three men walking along the mist-shrouded cliff-top, black on grey, towards us, it didn't take too much imagination to see again the movements of the first settlers here who built their crude Neolithic village on the shore at Scara Brae, or buried their dead in a burial cairn at Maes Howe, or erected that huge and mysterious henge of free-standing stones in a dandelion meadow which is the Ring of Brodgar. The stones are here still, defiant in their pre-paredness to stand there for all time and telling us something of men and women at their most primitive, and yet most spiritual, as they set up their own little bridges to distant gods whom they believed to be moving through the rainbows and mists all around them.

Then came the brilliant and fiery Norse who colonized these islands and used them as a base to launch bloody attacks on such as the Welsh princes on Anglesey. It was at these times that we see the first stirrings of Christianity since, as the Norse were sacking the Welsh, a young nobleman called Magnus refused to join in the pillaging, actually staying on the raiding ship and singing psalms if you please. Magnus's head was chopped off in the end since the times were not yet right for such revolutionary ideas of peace and love, but with his death the islands acquired their first Christian martyr and the fine red stone cathedral in Kirkwall is named after him.

Irish immigrants pitched up here, along with the odd Spanish sailor who may well have survived one shipwreck and was pretty sure he was not going to survive another. The Picts fought their way in as well and, out of this heady Celtic brew, a common faith began emerging which led to the building of one of the first Christian chapels in Europe here at Deerness. We all stood near the ruin, listening to the haunting silence and looking around at the sheer emptiness of these weeping Orkney skies.

This damp rubble would have been one of the first places of worship for the Celts; here they would have rooted their lives in the pioneering and experimental notions of purity and innocence while also making the first connections with a God who was the God of all things. 'He lights the light of the sun,' St Patrick had told them. 'He furnishes the light of the light. He has put springs in the dry land and has set stars to minister to the greater lights.'

With the aid of such teachings by the early saints the human, the natural and the divine were woven together in people's minds with a fresh intimacy and sense of wonder. The river became a place of baptism and regeneration; the mountain became a place of isolation and fervent prayer; and even the flapping, squawking wild geese became the early symbols of the Holy Spirit, the very arm of God's power with which he performed his mighty deeds.

The constant and changing revelations of light on these islands would have contained their own spiritual secrets since here also be angels. The Celtic mind believed in the reality of personal angels or heavenly beings who, as emissaries of God, patrolled their assigned territories watching over the fortunes of believers. You could all but see the wings of angels in those misty banks of rainbowed light; stare hard enough and that might even be Michael, the great archangel himself, swooping down with sword in hand and putting his many angelic troops on red alert.

The simplicity of structure of this chapel at Deerness tells us something of the way in which the early Celts had moved decisively away from the elaborate ceremonies and hierarchies of Rome where everything, even the bridges and triumphal arches in the streets, is about ten times bigger and fancier than anything you have ever seen before. You might even get a thousand of these chapels into St Peter's Church in Rome. But Italy does have an influence here, since there is a lovely little chapel nearby looking out over Scapa Flow built by Italian prisoners of war in 1943 and in service still.

The Celtic faith was always more mystical and a good deal more anarchic than Rome's. On the matter of when Easter fell, for example, the Celts took the view that if the Pope wanted it on a certain date then he could have it – they always respected Rome as a holy place – but they were going to take a date which better suited their own habits of fasting and abstaining from sex.

So, in the drifting Orkney mists all around us, we could perhaps see something of the primary colours and ideas of the Celtic Church; not in any great structures but in this rubbled ruin and in the seals out there lolling with their pups on the tide-washed rocks and in the endless carolling of the skylark and the continual wash of all that rain which makes these fields so lush and green. Here a simple faith has seeped as deeply into the earth as the rain and here at Deerness our group came a little closer to ourselves; we had sensed something of the mystery and wonder of a common God who remains mysterious and wonderful still.

We left the Royal Hotel in Thurso early the next morning, following the twisting coast road down through Caithness and looking out at the dark and emblematic oil rigs sitting in the smoothly glittering North Sea. On the other side of us the mountains were bald and snow-streaked in places, their foothills dotted with thin pagodas of foxgloves. Electricity pylons trooped mindlessly and intrusively across the sides of some of the mountains while, riding high on the thermals, was a pair of eagles.

I had got to know these parts quite well in my Fleet Street days, when I was often sent up to report on the roughnecks and roustabouts of the North Sea oil industry who could always be relied on to provide lively copy. Only that morning, in the Royal Hotel, I had been chatting to a group of divers who were out here salvaging a huge pump which had been wrecked in a storm and sunk to the sea bed near Dounreay. They had been diving off a platform to get at the pump, slicing and blowing it up and hauling bits up to the surface. You just cannot leave such wreckage lying about as in the old days, it seems, and they had already got Greenpeace and Scottish Heritage badgering them to get a move on.

The divers had just got back from the night shift, since their work was always governed by the tides, and were worried by my questions, wondering if I was a tax man. I was also interested to discover that one of them was a female, since I had never come across a woman in all my investigations into North Sea oil. She did, it was true, seem to smoke and swear as profusely as her colleagues, but this has always been a male macho world of hard drink and the odd bouts of violence.

Yet Celtic women had never been domestic chattels either, merely staying at home and washing the man's bearskin. Abbess Hilda of Whitby ruled over a monastery of men and women with a rod of iron while warriors such as Boadicea were famous in both love and war. The women would also be peacemakers, often baring their bosoms in battle to calm the enemy down and indeed it was not until the sixth century that it was decreed that women need no longer fight in battle and were never to be struck or insulted. The biggest punishment a man could inflict on his wife was to strike her lightly beneath her shoulders with a light twig and that was only if she gave away his harp, cloak or cauldron. 'Oh darling you haven't given the damned cauldron away again have you? Don't you understand how much cauldrons cost?'

Not that any self-respecting woman, no matter how

authoritarian or tough, would have wanted to live in Nigg Bay in Ross and Cromarty, which we were just passing. I went there more than a few years back and found it to be almost a Wild West town with but one pub and two ladies doing a brisk trade in a caravan. The few buildings were so sparse and rickety you half expected Clint Eastwood to show up and start gunning everyone down at any moment. Indeed the roughnecks and roustabouts may well, for all I knew, have been busy re-enacting the bloody and endless fighting of the old Celtic tribes and it was a rare night in the pub when some head or other did not get a good crack.

I had been pursuing another story altogether in Nigg when I bumped into a short, beefy man with a broken nose and a broad smile that filled his face with a school-boy naughtiness. I recognized him as Ivor, a bouncer who, at one time or another, had worked on the door of almost every night club in my home city of Cardiff. He had been brought into Nigg, he explained, to keep order on the Highland Queen, a former Clyde pleasure steamer which was being used as accommodation for the men, and where the violence was so bad that the lounge had been renamed Madison Square Garden.

The men on board called him Ivor the Bounce, he told me, and since he had started work there he had knocked out twenty men in ten weeks. Each of his knuckles was cut or bruised and seven of his fingers had been badly scarred from disarming some of the wilder razor boys from Glasgow. 'Most of the men here are gentlemen,' Ivor said with a broad wink. 'But there are a few here who carry razors and even guns and we have to look after them. Most of the time I can talk them into going to bed after they've had a few drinks but there are some you can't and you have to have a go. The problem with Nigg is boredom. There's nothing for the men to do so they start drinking and getting on one another's nerves by living so close together. You can't live in conditions like these after a hard day's work without feeling irritation at the slightest provocation.'

Two youths I met said they were both fed up with the boredom and violence on the Highland Queen and, as soon as they had finished their ten-week course, they were going to leave Nigg – and fast.

In fact Ivor left Nigg – and fast – after my report on how Ivor the Bounce took on the Wild Men of Nigg appeared in the following Sunday's *Observer*. I have followed Ivor's career closely, since each phase simply gets more and more colourful, even if it is now on temporary hold because he is in prison. And it has always seemed to me that Ivor, with his undoubted qualities of physical bravery and outstanding courage, could well have made a real Celtic warrior who, complete with a cape made of animal skins, a horned helmet and a large axe would have made mincemeat out of any marauding Viking or Norseman unlucky enough to come marauding down his way.

I walked quietly through the Great Wood of Culloden the next day, enjoying the delicate patterning of the light in the leaves and the busy tangling of many roots. Wolves and wild boar would have once roamed this wood but today there was just me and a distant magpie.

I have always loved wandering deep in the heart of a wood where I have felt enfolded and protected in a way I rarely feel in our ever more dangerous streets. A walk in the woods is rather like putting on an old and much-loved glove. After about half an hour, I sat on the trunk of a fallen tree to rest. Next to me was a strange, sponge-like fungus, the size of a dinner plate, and the earth was alive with ants going about ant business.

In the next clearing a man in a ragged strip of cloth was tilling the earth where he was growing flax and hemp. A woman walked past stooping beneath a heavy load of bullrushes with which she was going to make a mat. All of us seem to have been living in this forest forever now; it is our own small world where we will always be kept safe from the nameless and formless terrors of the gigantic world outside; where we make love in the glades and sing hymns to the glory of life beneath these leaves.

I stood up from my fallen tree trunk and continued walking again, following a twisting path which seemed to be twisting nowhere at all. There were some fresh badger tracks down near a stream and bats were already out hunting above the trees, their flights fluttering this way and that as they snatched insects out of the air. Other creatures were clearly moving around inside the dark thickets of the wood too; even if I could not see them, I was sure they could see me.

But, fortunately, I never had to hunt these creatures since, as the artist of the tribe, it was my job to create art out of the world all around me. So I was keen to stand around here and study the way light moves through shadow, particularly at this time of the day when the very air seemed to be endowed with a real passion. The shapes of the trees are always interesting and there is a spirit deep within a forest which seems to pull everything together.

I have always been fascinated by this spirit of interconnectedness, which is why the knot is the basis of my designs. The knot pulls together everything and everyone: the pagan and the Christian, man and woman, life and death. I'm hoping to be making a large stone cross soon and again I'll be using a form of embroidery on it which will be interconnected in the same way as the forest and indeed all life. Such embroidery tells us it is in the shelter of one another that we all live. Together we prosper and apart we die. I also want my art to say something about the nature of God which I have perceived through my senses; something about his bigness and otherness and total unpredictability. My colours are selected carefully too: gold for royalty, green for nature and red for Christ's blood.

I walked into another clearing down by a river and came across the glowing splendour of a large fire which had been built by some Boy Scouts. It groaned and flamed and spat with a fine fury and the Scouts were standing at some distance from it, gazing at its deep, fierce heart with an almost primordial fascination.

Fires like this tell the world that we will never be overcome by darkness and that our inner spiritual fires will always continue to burn, even in the longest and darkest of our nights. Fires like this reflect both the destructive and purifying sides of God, and it would have been a fire exactly like this that St Patrick built on the Hill of Slane within sight of the palace of the High King of Tara. The High King claimed copyright on all fires in Ireland and, with this one thrilling act of defiance, the old saint served notice on him that the reign of the Druids, the soothsayers and all the other demons, which were so blighting life on an Irish earth, was over and a new age of Christianity had begun.

I moved closer to the fire and, on hearing the sounds of nickering horses, took one step back, looking from side to side. A strange shape seemed to be coming together inside the fire and I could not understand it. There were the sounds of creaking wheels and rattling reins when, with a long and terrifying roar, the fire fell apart and a great, golden chariot broke free from the waving flames with a huge white horse pulling it upwards at speed. The wheels whirled furiously and, with a crack of a whip, the chariot sailed over my head before turning this way and that, almost as if caught in a moment of indecision, before setting off, with a further series of cracked whips, in the direction of Jordan.

It was dusk and I was sitting on a low graveyard wall looking out over a winding valley with a river running through it. From somewhere distant and invisible a train was clanking to a halt and a man was walking past me carrying two bags bulging with shopping as swallows went skittering frantically through a mackerel sky. Further out there were the rooftops of this small Scottish city which had all the marvellous perfection of the ordinary. Beyond were green fields dotted with yellow parallelograms of oil seed rape.

The shops here were like the shops everywhere else; the gardens were like everyone else's and even the wall on which I was sitting had lots of metal stumps on it, after the iron railings had been shorn off to help in the war effort. Just like everyone else's.

But this veneer of the ordinary concealed a heart riven with the purest pain. You could actually feel this pain on every street corner and the anguish seemed to have drenched every house and tree and sat, a silent and unbidden guest, on every hearth. I was sitting on the graveyard wall of Dunblane Cathedral, entering the suffering of the Scottish people who were lamenting the deaths of sixteen children and one teacher who, six months ago, had been shot in their school gymnasium by Thomas Hamilton, yet another murderous maniac of our video age.

The Celtic Heart has always been especially close to suffering; the Welsh even have a word for it, *dwysder*, which, although it has no exact counterpart in English, means the consciousness of a mighty burden – those times when we become lost in the long, dark nights of the soul. The Irish began to learn about suffering without end during the famine; a feeling which has since been reinforced almost daily for the past thirty years during the Troubles in the North. We Welsh also received the hardest shock under heaven when a coal tip exploded and

37

came crashing down on a small school in Aberfan in 1966, killing 116 children and twenty-eight adults. I was there that morning and entered as deeply as anyone into the suffering of my people.

But that tip did not just crash into that school and those poor children; it crashed into all our lives and certainties, made an incomprehensible and untreatable wound in our sides and even struck, with devastating force, at our very faith. I mean to say if children cannot go to school and be kept safe then what is going on? Where was the hand of God in all this? And thus began a long, dark night of the Welsh soul from which many have yet to emerge. The bitterness is even inscribed into the tombstones in Aberfan cemetery: Why did you have to break our hearts by taking our best? Why?

Now it was the turn of the Scots to come to terms with senseless tragedy and, six months on, they were still crying as they kept coming back to this wonderful cathedral in Dunblane, with its ravishing stained glass and glorious oak carvings of sorrowing angels, all looking for a healing and release which seems as distant as ever. They still shy away from strangers like frightened animals and the mere mention of 'that school' makes them fall silent. Yes, these are the days of a new heartbreak without end all right; a heartbreak with no remission or time off for good behaviour.

I went up to the local cemetery that afternoon to pay my respects to the children who were lying there together with lots of fresh flowers and their favourite toys and teddy bears. They have chosen a high, grassy site and, on each grave, a tiny toy windmill was clicking softly and unbearably in the breeze. As I walked away from the graves, my tearful eyes met those of a woman coming up the hill carrying flowers; a newly bereaved mother, I knew, who looked away sharply, unable to cope with whatever it was that she saw in my own eyes.

In the school there were tubs of flowers where the gymnasium of death once stood. Remember us in your prayers, the colourful and grimly smiling flowers said. We may not be with you bodily but we will live in your broken hearts forever. They have built a shrine of sorts to the lost children of Dunblane inside the cathedral, a corner of teddy bears and notes from people the world over declaring that they are there with them and asking the one big question: Why?

'There was a gun club near us and they used to meet every Sunday morning,' one woman wrote on a postcard. 'They observed a service of remembrance for the children, fired one shot and I have not heard them since.'

As I watched the sky darkening over Dunblane it seemed to be darkening in another sense too; darkening with a spirit of murderous evil which was spreading over the rest of the world. These gun massacres were now happening everywhere with a sickening regularity and your heart could but chill and your stomach churn as you thought about where this evil might be coming from and considered who or what might be responsible for its spread.

Midges rose in the thin orange glow of eventide like a thousand tiny angels preparing to do battle and there was damp confetti lying in the graveyard grass reminding us of old joys. Some of the gravestones were tilting this way and that in the time-honoured manner, and there was a memorial obelisk to William McCann who fought for the Union in the American Civil War.

As the shadows kept lengthening I heard again the clicking of all those toy windmills in a corner of Scotland that would forever be grief. Then something sharper rode the winds; an unbearable cry of pain; a long keening which wept for children who had died years too soon and I knew – I just knew – that here in a land where the shadows were becoming so thick and cold that the rays of the sun were no longer able to penetrate them; here where even the birds were becoming afraid to fly and music was no longer able to lift the heart, Deirdre of the Sorrows, that old Celtic heroine whose name had become a byword for tragedy, was still very much alive and crying still.

4

Balor in Bog of Allen

———

THE BOAT'S ENGINE screamed furiously as it drove up against the huge wave then screamed even louder as it crested the high roller before plummeting directly down again. This was a white-knuckle ride and no messing, just the three of us clinging grimly to the silver handrails as the boat went screaming up the back of another wave and down the next. Spray stung our faces and our shouted words were swept away by the sea winds.

The boat soared almost vertically again and, in the quiet yet sustained fury all around, my heart trampolined a bit when I finally saw them close up – the Skelligs, two ragged triangles of rock rising up out of the swelling seas. These islands were among the loneliest and most inaccessible places of pilgrimage in all Ireland and it was in locations like this that the early Celts first learned the holy laws of a holy God.

In winter it is all but impossible to get to the Skelligs even on fine days. Now in the early autumn the boat was on its first trip there for four days but our skipper Joe Roddy had not been too happy about doing this. The winds picked up again as we lurched towards the smaller Skellig, disturbing thousands of gannets who rose up and wheeled around our heads in swirling, gabbling clouds. Big-eyed seals basked on one rock and, the nearer we got to the island, the more powerful was the smell of the faeces of the 24,000 nesting birds there, the second largest gannetry in the world. The guano had stained the brown

41

rocks a dark green with long dribbles of dirty white. My particular favourites, the puffins, had long gone by this time of year, away roaming the North Atlantic looking for sand eels.

We headed for the larger Skellig Michael, whose massive splintered outline towered over us. Joe jumped onto the small stone quay and steadied our boat as we scrambled ashore. The seas around us were deep and black and some of those huge swells would have travelled thousands of miles after being set rolling by some distant depression. Silence engulfed us almost as soon as we began climbing up those steep, campion-speckled slopes.

Many parts of Ireland are totally bereft of silence. Every minute of every hour brings a solid wall of pop music; every opening door and window lets loose a gale of Radio One; even sleeping in a camper van in the middle of a moorland often provides no escape from passing transistors. But here, at last, was the authentic sound of silence broken only by the suck and wash of those deep black waves on the rocks below.

Joe, broad of girth and ruddy of complexion, struggled up the crumbling rock steps in front of us. 'This climb never gets any easier,' he puffed. We climbed up another set of steps and, high up in the gently squalling winds, we came across what we had been looking for: an old stone oratory – a small place of worship perched there and looking out over the heaving sea.

I could see Finian, the old monk who had originally set up this hermitage with five others, down on his knees in there, with his head bowed and praising God. He was a man of iron will who took a child's delight in designing and building the small stone buildings on this island with little more than his hands and the stones which littered the slopes. He was a fine man, this Finian, and nothing ever bothered him. If there was no food available he starved; if there was no fresh water he went without. He taught that something was bound to turn up. No harm could ever befall anyone in a state of holiness, he said.

Even to sign up for the original monastery a prospective monk had to learn the psalms off by heart. When he was in, he had to recite the lot, aloud, three times a day to the winds and the birds. Yes, there is a powerful, dreaming holiness about this place, that's for sure. But all islands mediate the concept of holiness to us. They are pure, inviolate and lonely, where you can reach out and touch the hand of God without any intervening walls. All the saints of old sought out such islands; they found the very centres of their being on places like this.

We climbed yet higher and Joe was puffing a lot more when we got to the monastery itself with its six beehive huts, two oratories, lots of weather-scarred crosses and a slightly pathetic graveyard, no bigger than a small flower-bed, where the monks had been buried. The weather had worn their tombstones down to gnarled stumps and, from the very smallness of the plot, you would never be able to guess how many monks were buried there.

'We have no records of their daily lives, so a lot of what we know is pure conjecture,' said Michael Grimes, a student working for the Office of Public Works on the island. 'But we do know that the early Christians were always attracted to the seclusion of the island and desert. They believed that they should become exiles for Christ.'

As he spoke you could feel the ghosts of those flinty, psalm-chanting monks slippering through the air all around you. Their lives were the hardest ever with an almost continual struggle to find fresh water which they had to barter from passing ships. They offered salted gannets or sacks of feathers. Guillemot eggs were sometimes enough for a barrel of water or a small pile of my beloved puffins. But those monks did not last long. Few of them reached the age of forty and, when they fell ill, they died, and were buried on top of one another right there.

43

Their hard life became considerably harder in the eighth century when the Vikings, in their passing longships, began taking an interest in the hermitage. 'Bitter is the wind; it tosses the waves' white hair,' one monk wrote in the margin of a manuscript he had been working on. 'I fear the Norse warriors are riding the sea outside.'

What could anyone do about these men who kept coming back again and again like starving tigers, propelled by the strangest and most evil ideas known to man? Their only way to Valhalla, they believed, was through pillaging and war. Their only kingdom was their ship and they could never sleep under a proper roof, let alone ever enjoy the community of a family around the hearth. Show a Viking a child and, far from showing it love, all he could think of doing was running a spear through it. Try and offer him the hand of friendship and he would cut it off.

The monks finally left in the thirteenth century and this island became a famous centre for pilgrimage and penitence. Pilgrims were expected to do the nerve-wracking Stations of the Cross around the jutting rocks then crawl out and kiss a stone slab overhanging the sea at Needle's Eye. Only one pilgrim ever fell off and died but he was said to have been an atheist so it did not matter. Some pilgrims got carried away and actually began partying here, said Joe. Apparently they were singing and dancing and carrying on so much that the mainland police had to be called to clear them off.

Yet these great poems in stone soon came to define the meaning of isolation and we kept looking around us at those shifting silences, and marvelling that a faith could flourish in such an unpromising place as this. The sun was sinking towards the horizon and we had to get back down to our boat. Long bursts of light were breaking up in the shadows as we followed the path down to the jetty. Yet again I fancied that I glimpsed the mighty archangel Michael, after whom this rock had been named, gliding down out of the sunset with his great sword raised, except that the moving light moved again and, with a swoosh of his wings, Michael was gone.

There is a real freedom in travelling through a country in a camper van because, when the fancy takes you, you can just pull into a dark car park, eat something or make yourself a cup of tea, and then curl up in your sleeping bag until the morning. Pubs generally do not mind you sleeping in their back yards, as long as you ask, and there is nothing quite like waking up on a river bank, when the sun is climbing up the blue back of the morning, and sitting on a chair outside your own back door, watching the river and all that moves in it, with but a prayer in your mind and a hymn in your heart.

But sometimes you yearn for the luxury of a proper bed with crisp cotton sheets, and a deep warm bath, with – my very favourite sensation of them all – lots of crystals crunching under your bum as you lower yourself into it. So, from time to time, I do shell out a vast amount of money to stay in a proper hotel, which I did in Limerick, only to realize that I had made a big and expensive mistake.

My first inkling that a strange drama was about to be played out around me came when I opened my hotel bedroom door and saw a man, like Mr Bean, sitting with his trousers down around his ankles, on my lavatory. 'Excuse me,' he said.

'No, excuse me,' I replied withdrawing in confusion.

A chambermaid emerged in the corridor and apologized, saying that there had been a mistake and, within a minute or so, I had been relocated into a rather marvellous suite with everything one could ever hope for, including fresh flowers and a deep marble bath for which I had big plans. Was this all right for sir? Ah yes, it was, it was.

I was about to wash my socks, which were stinking and

dancing about together, when there was a knock on my door. A woman, who might have been the manageress, said she was sorry but this suite was booked tonight so would I mind going back to my original room?

I did mind but I went anyway and saw that, by now, Mr Bean had disappeared but, unfortunately, his stink had not. The room was like a gas chamber and I raced across it to try and fling open the windows, except that there was something wrong with the catch and the windows kept closing again. 'I can't stay in this,' I gasped with my eyes watering.

'Neither could I,' said the manageress who, sensibly, was standing outside in the corridor.

My next bedroom turned out to be above a pedestrian crossing with bells going off every time a pedestrian crossed. This was almost bearable but a shop alarm went off next door and rang non-stop for almost an hour. More than ready for suicide I rang reception and begged for another room.

By now I had moved five times but this one was not too bad except for the man singing in the next bedroom, 'something' moaning inside the central heating, and distant sounds which might have been coming from a nearby cinema. To get a cup of tea you had to go to the landing at the end of the corridor and make your own. This was quite difficult since the kettle was firmly manacled to the wall with one of the biggest and thickest chains I have ever seen. The chain made it impossible to pour any hot water into the cup and, as there were no teaspoons, I had to use my door key, attached to a huge wooden knob, to stir the tea.

There was no hot water for any crystal-crunching in the bath or any to wash or shave. When I approached the manager the next morning, ready to deliver a whole litany of complaint, he was unwilling to discuss anything with me. But he did cancel my bill, perhaps believing that was apology enough.

At least the whole episode gave me a renewed appreciation of my beautiful camper which, I realized there and then, comes with the distinct added advantage that, if anywhere gets too noisy, all I have to do is wriggle out of my sleeping bag, jump into the driving seat and drive like mad until I find a patch of silence again.

Limerick has long had a reputation for shadiness and violence – many call it Stab City – but, while it does not have any of Dublin's Georgian elegance, I found it welcoming and friendly, even when I attended a meeting of Alcoholics Anonymous there that night, as we alcoholics are always told to do when we are under any extreme stress, as I had felt immediately I got into Dingle, and whenever I stayed in strange hotels.

It was in a school and we all sat in small desks in front of a blackboard as the members shared their sad tales of dereliction and destruction with their usual appalling honesty: the thieving, the bed-wetting, the sheer wanton vandalism of mind and heart. It was all there being told in the same way as I had heard similar stories being told in meetings in almost every part of the world.

St Paul used to talk a lot about the fellowship of suffering in which people nourish and revive one another in times of hardship. The early Christians needed such fellowship in that first savage era of Roman rule but there was something even deeper than that at work in this fellowship. What was going on here was that each of the members were constantly reinforcing one another's sobriety with like-minded ideas. It is our ideas that almost alone rule our world and our view of ourselves and, if these ideas become contaminated, then so do we. Ideas are like viruses which can work for good or evil. Change your ideas and you immediately change yourself.

I do not suppose that there was anything particularly Irish – or even Celtic – about many of their stories, even

47

if I had long noticed that there were many Irish Catholics in the fellowship. Alcoholism is a worldwide disease, chopping down everyone regardless of their nationality or background. Yet as the 'shares' continued I began to understand how alcohol had become another resident demon in so many Irish lives and I wondered if this demon could even be responsible for more death and despair in this country than the combined efforts of Oliver Cromwell, the Black and Tans, the B-Specials and all the current terror gangs put together. Demons do not need to be in any particular size or shape, and the truly vicious feature of this one was that he actually poisoned you while making you feel better at the same time.

There was lots of laughter in the meeting, with frequent references to God – or 'our Higher Power' as he is often known. There had been a strong Christian conscience in many of them, I guessed, before it had been lost in drink. The Irish even had their own 'patron saint' of alcoholics, Matt Talbot; a Dublin soak who had sobered up after seeing a vision on a bridge.

Early the next morning I decided to follow water into the heart of Ireland, setting out from Limerick along the banks of the mighty Shannon and past a ruined castle. The rising sun clung to the water, making it shiver in silvery patches, and lots of seagulls were sitting together on the water next to a sewage outlet. The river was flowing fast, engorged by recent downpours of rain. In the summer it can dawdle and dance but today its flow was as silent as it was big, as it hurried to make an urgent appointment somewhere deep in the Atlantic.

The brown autumnal leaves had begun falling, spinning this way and that slowly in the faint breezes until they hit the water, whereupon they became the fastest speedboats. On one bend there was the outline of a sunken car and there were wheel tracks where it appeared to have been driven down the bank. Every now and then a sleek, silver aeroplane sliced through the skies before droning in low to land at Shannon airport.

I was entering the lower Shannon floodlands, a wondrous kingdom of patchworked water meadow where the river always floods at this time of year, reclaiming the land on which farmers grow their hay in summer. The river is unusually large for a country this size, rising in a distant coal field then taking water from the rivers and springs of six counties until it all comes together around here and debouches over yet another coalfield. These rolling floodlands, some one hundred thousand acres of water meadow, erupt out of a huge gutter which was once quarried by the slow and relentless interplay between hot sun and cold ice. Here they became water meadows, colonized by many songbirds and dotted with purple and yellow loosestrife.

Such water wonderlands are the very cradle of the Celts and, just being here, with the whole ancient music of old Erin seeping out of all these rolling artefacts of light, I began stumbling and slipping through the thickets of Irish history again, seeing a sky full of hunting peregrines or parachuting skylarks. The water meadows were thick with geese and swans while the nights were full of the calls of the corncrake or the drumming of snipe. Thick oak forests once covered those bare hills where kings like Brian Boru took refuge when he was not attacking the Danes.

The story of the whole race lies on these banks and, spotting the ruins of an old ironworks, I could work out that those oak trees had been felled for the smelting process. Those tall, pencil-shaped stone towers were once the home of insecure fifteenth-century chieftains and over there was the burial tomb of a Stone Age farmer.

The ruins of those forgotten villages call up the desperate famine years and my heart was broken again – just as it was broken a million times over and over – as I saw

49

again the wretched mud cabins and heard again the piteous groans of all those starving people and smelled again the loathsome stench of all those filthy workhouses with the idiot cells and fever sheds which were but nurseries for cholera and typhus. And I could taste again those horrid India maize meals doled out in the soup kitchens ... oh enough of this ... enough ...

The villages around here were also at the forefront of the fight against absentee English landlords when burly bailiffs would arrive in force to evict those who would not – or could not – pay their rent. Sick people were hauled out of their beds as priests anxiously begged the mobs not to resort to violence. Doors were smashed in and complete roofs taken off. Ah yes, with my own Celtic Heart I suffered along with them, and entered into their pain and anguish. The Celtic experience has been built on one huge altar of pain.

Darkness was falling, along with a thin drizzle, as I approached the small town of Killaloe, a scattering of stone houses around a thin thirteen-arched bridge on a loch, sentinelled by the Slieve mountains on one side and the Arra mountains on the other. The locals here have always enjoyed water and they once had a saint here, Molhua, who, in all justice, should have been a tadpole since he was never happier than when swimming near that long bridge.

Molhua was a contemporary of Brendan, another water enthusiast, who was forever jumping into some alarmingly fragile craft and sailing off into the wide blue yonder. Neither of them could sit still on terra firma for more than five minutes when their eyes and thoughts would be wandering in the direction of water. Brendan, we may remember, made a spectacular and dangerous voyage to the Land of the Promise. Seven years that voyage took, becoming, in the end, a story that has lived in the folk memory of the world. The Celts were always great wanderers; turn your back and they were off.

Apart from a few pubs and the odd hotel Killaloe had a pleasant, if small, cathedral, built out of yellow and blue sandstone and in the shape of a cross. Next to it was St Flannan's Oratory, a crude stone structure, and it was near there I parked up for the night, worming down into my sleeping bag and beginning a long and elaborate dream in purple.

It was dark and I was lying on one of those wooden ski jumps in the middle of the loch when I caught sight of half a dozen dark angels flying together through a ragged moonscape above the Slieve mountains. Then I saw something infinitely more ominous taking shape above the Arra mountains, since it looked as if half a dozen searchlights were floating up into the skies before coming together and forming a solid wall of purple light.

In the confused and frightening circumstances, I decided to slip into the water and duck under the ski jump, watching the wall of light get ever brighter as it moved towards me. The strange feature of this wall was that I could not see how it was being held up or illuminated. Rather like an angel it did not seem to have a proper size, since it was just hanging there with its huge purple glow dissipating the darkness.

The wall did not seem to attract the attention of the dark angels as it passed directly over me and on up to the Shannon. But then it stopped and began moving back towards me. Still unsure of what was going on, I decided to dive full fathom five although, as I began getting close to the loch floor, it became apparent that, despite all the known laws of physics, the wall of purple light had reached down here and was now engulfing me as I swam around inside it like a lost goldfish. I darted forward but the light held me. I flashed sideways but still I was held in that purple orb. This was not my idea of a joke.

The way it developed was almost beyond language.

There were boats and hands and soft voices. Everything was blurred as I was passed from one pair of hands to the next. Everything was going on in a slurping underwater silence and, apart from the purple, the only other colour was black. Long black arms reached out and rolled me along a purple bed. I was picked up again and now purple arms began rolling over a black bed. Black to purple, purple to black. Colours moved seamlessly into one another in this purple and black rhapsody.

The next minute I was being lowered down through the water and laid to rest on the deck of a boat with crystal ropes and an ox-hide hull. Breezes filled up the sails and the ropes hummed with tension as I was ferried across the trackless purple water. An albatross circled overhead and flying fish were breaking away from the hull. Finally, masses of black hands picked me up again, carrying me ashore to an island which, although small, had seven churches on it. The churches were not conventionally designed, yet the altar candles pierced the night with such vivacity they made the buildings float on a bed of pure light.

All around me was the hum of worship with the soft sounds of bells marking off the hours and the quiet surges of Gregorian chant. More bells heralded the start of Compline. Monks were packing the choirstalls and a single candle was burning on the altar which the monks kept circling. The abbot, St Caimin, sprinkled each monk with holy water and I caught some of the stray splashes with which I washed my eyes.

The purple light began fading into pure sunlight which, in its turn, revealed the full majesty of a great working monastery. There might have been 300 monks here and a large group walked straight past me reading their morning office together. I reached out to one of them to discover if he was real – which he was.

The sound of the bells quickened, the one peal running straight into the other. A huge dark cloud blotted out the sunlight and lumps of masonry began falling off the walls. Weeds grew out of the walls as the cloister windows became thick with cobwebs. Siren winds kept blowing with an Arctic sorrow as I finally awoke in a cold, forbidding and empty dawn in my camper van in Killaloe.

Winter was finally putting the land under her relentless clamp when I left Mountshannon harbour, following the Grand Canal which was going to take me into Dublin. Nothing moved on the still water, with the lock gates closed and the pleasure craft tarpaulined and moored together. The water itself was muddy and brown, revealing little of the fish who live and swim in it. This same canal was once used to service the giant Guinness filter beds outside Dublin, giving the stout its distinctive flavour but, quite frankly, you really should not drink this water even if you are dying of thirst. That thick brown colour comes from suspended turf, since this water rises deep in the vast black bowels of the Bog of Allen.

But you can spot flashes of leggy herons or even wild mink as you poke around between the lock gates. Mink are the nastiest, most murderous things on four legs. They do not like to eat a lot nor do they store anything away for a rainy day. Mink murder so much because they are psychopaths who love killing for the sake of it.

The main commercial activity on the canal is now pleasure cruisers, but they do not operate in the winter. Near Edenderry I went to see Heather and Michael Thomas who have been running Celtic Canal Cruisers for the past twenty-three years. Originally they bought a small ruined house by the canal and started out with two boats for rent. They now have fifteen boats which chug back and forth along the seventy-five miles of canal between here and Dublin. But canal holidaymakers are not in any real danger as they might be at sea, since most of them could stand up in the canal which is never more than five feet deep.

The occupying British army used the canal regularly to send their troops down this way to put down pockets of belligerence in the West. At least a hundred thousand people used this canal to escape the famine and get to the soup kitchens of Dublin all those years ago. Oh here we go again. That famine is almost everywhere you look isn't it? I sometimes find that I can look at the smallest thing like the way the ropes of the canal barges have cut into the sides of that bridge and the whole sickening misery of the famine comes flaring up again.

They had to put an armed guard on some of the canal boats which were carrying food. Starving people besieged these boats when they were being unloaded but they rarely managed to make off with so much as a mouldy carrot. 'The Rudeness, Wickedness, love of Mischief and inclination to injure public works is so strongly imbibed in almost every Creature of the lower Class that it will require the utmost care in the Bridge keeper to protect his Charge,' said a contemporary report.

Darkness was spreading over the countryside but the canal water held a slight orange glow as I followed the tow path into Tullamore, the county town of Offaly. This town used to be the start of the canal into Dublin while raging arguments took place for many years on how, exactly, the canal might be extended to the banks of the Shannon. For a while they settled on this place as the final harbour and that quay was once the home of D. E. Williams, distillers of the famous and potent Tullamore Dew and Irish Mist whiskey.

Canal trips from Tullamore were popular days out in the 1800s. But no one 'in liquor' could get on the boats and those behaving in an 'indecent and disorderly manner' would be bounced off. Houses along the canal sold drink to the passengers and the crews were often fined for being drunk or playing cards with the passengers. The seventy-eight-mile trip, with fifty-six lock-keepers from Dublin to Shannon, cost thirteen shillings for a state cabin and eight shillings for a rougher variety. The boats travelled at about four miles an hour and it was, in fact, far quicker to walk, although a lot more strenuous.

This part of the canal was the stamping ground of another Celtic saint, Manchan, who was not exactly peculiar except that he had an extreme reverence for his cow. Anyway, some rascal pinched his cow one day and the poor beast duly ended up in a boiling cauldron. Manchan was livid and put a curse on everyone in the area insisting that, in future, any traveller in these parts could always claim a free drink of milk from anyone, no matter what the time of day or night. Some still try it, I have heard, but they are not always successful because the locals insist on such a colossal deposit on the bottle. There are, as they say, no flies on the good people of Offaly.

It was a singular, riven place this Bog of Allen, with lots of low black contours and long, plastic-draped ridges in the parts that were being mined for peat and lots of heavy duty machinery standing around like giant behemoths frozen there for all time.

I found a deserted corner to stay the night, revelling in the blackness all around me and then brooding on it, knowing there was something dark and desperate washing around deep inside this bog. But what quite?

We know that nothing washes around inside bogland peat, which is made up of the dead remains of trees, marsh plants and other mosses which have been crushed together for thousands of years. People in the Iron Age clearly understood the preservative qualities of this oxygen-free peat, since they used it as a sort of early safe to bury their jewellery and the corpses of men who had been ritually murdered. They are all down there still, togged out in their funereal, deerskin capes and around their necks the bands of willow rods which had strangled them.

What is not generally known is that there is a huge ocean of surging malignity inside these bogs which makes them especially dangerous and unstable. I wandered out into the twilight and listened hard, actually able to hear all the pained rumblings which were especially eloquent on the subject of grief. A lot of people have committed suicide in this bog and many more have been ritually murdered here, all attracted by that same siren song of grief.

There is cannibalism here too, since everything feeds on everything else in the bog; everything, that is, except the bog cotton which manages to keep going by feeding on its own decaying issues.

Darkness came and I could never remember seeing such darkness. Vast black patches of worked bog moved into yet more vast black patches of worked bog. With the aid of the overhanging clouds which blocked out the moon, this bog seemed to have managed the remarkable feat of draining every last particle of light out of the air. Yes, this was the darkest of the dark all right. Paint the whole lot black.

I heard a malign wave again, roaring upwards, but collapsing back on itself in anger and disappointment after it had been unable to find a fault in the earth. Faults mean release and release means volcano. This was the way the internal syllogism hung together, deep in the Bog of Allen.

Something else moaned a mile or so down again when the very peat seemed to be breaking up with tiny speckles of green light bobbing and drifting all around like millions of courting fireflies. A giant figure began articulating in this huge, green glow, limb by limb and feature by feature, a figure that was like nothing that I had ever seen. He had a shield over one shoulder and was holding a spear. He also had only one eye.

Ah yes, I knew who this was; this was Balor of the Baleful Eye, King of the Formorians, a vicious Celtic pirate and long-standing enemy of the Irish.

That eye was so big, it has been written somewhere, that it took three men with scaffolding and pulleys to lift it. There was certainly no friendliness in it and, as he moved closer to me, I could see what an extraordinary creation it was: it seemed to pick up and hold everything in its huge lens.

Lots of strange and alien movements were taking place around the pink iris. I saw figures that I did not recognize: a tall, blonde figure holding an ice-pick in her hand, a muscular gunman with a bandolier of ammunition criss-crossing his chest, and a pack of hunting, fighting dogs. I also saw windows being smashed in that eye and two gangs attacking one another with iron bars and baseball bats. There was the surging arc of a hurled petrol bomb and the distant sound of an explosion. Not all the imagery in that eye was violent. There were also films of sparkling new cars and shapely models parading on tropical beaches. Violence mixed with entertainment and consumerism in about equal measure. So this is what the enemy of the Irish looked like these days and I could only stand there dumbfounded with puzzlement.

Balor hoisted his spear aloft as if he was about to throw it at me, so I picked up a stone and, with all my strength, threw it directly into his massive eye. The stone disappeared straight into the pink iris and caused a huge bang as the eye exploded into thousands of shards of flying glass.

Some of the shards cut into my face and I could still feel the pinpricks of pain in my cheeks the next morning when I looked out into a dew-covered dawn with a stray sheet of plastic being blown around the bog slowly in a slight breeze. Further out again were the pylons and cooling towers of a power station.

I was exhausted and felt that I had had no sleep when I located that canal again, wanting to get to Dublin as soon as possible. There were a lot more of those new bungalows around here; all rather different from the crude huts that once lined this canal, as I remember: ragged squares built out of muddy sods with roofs thatched out of bullrushes and potato stalks. Such food as they had could not be cooked properly since fuel was often a problem. On extremely cold days in the winter of the famine whole families would huddle together for warmth, sometimes joined by neighbours or passers-by.

There were the times when some of those people became swollen with typhus and were so fevered and hot that they would run screaming to the canal and jump into the water to cool down. Rickets entered their blood in the shape of small needles and gave them terrible muscular spasms. When they were taken with dropsy their muscles would actually burst. Oh here I was at it again ... those were the times to forget if only you ever could ... and now I was suffering from prickly pains in my own face, wondering where they had come from.

5

A Mad Blonde at St David's

I TOOK THE ROAD out of Haverfordwest, passing damp fields and haphazard lines of white and orange traffic cones. A bunch of sparrows were sitting on the high wires of the electricity pylons, making me wonder yet again why they did not turn into feathered toast, and then I was swooping down into Newgale where the waves kept surging in and making the whole pebble beach rattle like so many balls in a giant game of bingo.

The small coastal town of Solva came and went before I accelerated down into the smallest city of them all, St David's in west Wales, with fewer than 2,000 inhabitants. St David's could be a small Welsh village anywhere with terraces lining the main street and the odd pockets of frying chips or stewing tea. A cat with glittering silver eyes was sitting in a front window watching the passers-by. An old lady in a brown coat and carrying a blue bag was frowning hard as she struggled to walk against the wishes of her arthritis or whatever else was clogging up her legs.

The cathedral was not yet visible as I sauntered down the main street but there was something very special in the air which has always tasted to me as if it had been freshly baked by angels. This place is a spiritual power point in the same, if undefinable, way as Glastonbury or Lindisfarne. There's a clean feeling of heaven here which seems to throb up out of the streets. A spirit of healing has been woven into this throbbing – and the sweet smell of holiness.

St David, the patron saint of Wales, in whose home town I was walking, is a key figure in the Welsh spiritual psyche. In a sense he was the godfather of us all and, if you want to know what the Welsh really believe in, you merely have to look at his life and works. He taught us how to pray and worship. By his own impeccable example he showed us how to frame our lives around hard work and abstinence. Almost more than anyone else he showed us that religion was not an enslavement but a freedom. He is as alive today as he was when he grew up in the fields around here, a giant, charismatic man, famous for his asceticism, preaching and miracles. Doves sat on his shoulder and became his management consultants. His logo was the daffodil. He was the Waterman, seven feet tall and reckoned to be 147 when he died on 1 March 589, proving that, if you want to live a long life, you should work hard, pray hard and drink nothing stronger than water.

A huge stone cross stood at the end of the main road with a couple of skinheads sitting on its base sharing a flagon of cider. Further on I passed a bookshop and went through an arch to look down on the roof of the cathedral, deliberately built in this deep hollow so that it would not be visible to pirates out at sea. Next to the cathedral was the broken-jawed ruin of the Bishop's Palace, now the home of lots of noisy jackdaws whose cracked, staccato calls could be heard along the outlying valley.

Back in the fifth century many rainbows began building up along the nearby coastline, heralding the arrival of a new holy man. This was a holy man like no other, the rainbow seemed to be saying. This was going to be a marvellous new prophet, a new riddle hatched deep in the mind of God.

A mile or so from here was the holy well which marks the spot where St Non gave birth to this new prophet. It is a bleakly beautiful spot which can give you severe shortage of breath. On the one side rocks stand around in the boiling sea in various stages of disarray and, on the other, there is the low, lush spin of hills and green fields. These parts become especially noisy one day in early autumn, when the skies blacken as more than a million birds fly overhead – skylarks, chaffinches and blackbirds – all with their bags packed and squeals of joy in their beaks as they head off for their winter hols in the sunshine of Brazil or Spain.

After leaving here to work in other countries David returned to this, his beloved kingdom of Menevia, setting up a community and introducing Opus Dei, a daily round of ordered worship. He fought demons and healed children, rebuilding the true faith anew in a land riddled with such heresies as Pelagianism and torn by tornadoes carrying plague germs. His work did nothing less than usher in the first golden age of the Celtic Church.

Nona Rees, the cathedral librarian, lives in Treasury Cottage next to the cathedral with her children, a daft dog and a rook with an attitude problem. She has written a lot about St David and says that he will live in the minds of the Welsh forever. 'He has never been a cypher but someone who lives to this day,' she said. 'He spoke Welsh and, like Christ, was a real historical figure. Everyone is still aware of what he stood for.'

All the figures of this first great Celtic period gathered strange and miraculous myths around them and David was no exception. One story-teller even claimed that David had invented rugby by picking up stones in the field and flinging them into touch when he was trying to plough it. Other stories tell of how he turned water into wine or raised the dead. 'He was the cultural Clint Eastwood of the Dark Ages,' said a director of Celtic tourism. 'He brought stability and learning to communities which had become as torn apart as the roughest and most violent places in the Wild West.'

Well Clint Eastwood he wasn't since, first and last, David was a law-abiding ascetic who hardly went around the place toting a .44 Magnum. David wore animal skins and walked everywhere barefoot, insisting that his followers did the same. He drank only water and ate only bread and vegetables, advocating a life of unremitting hard work. He never lost his temper but could be resolutely bloody-minded, particularly when dealing with the bullying local chieftains or other assorted pagan barbarians who tried to make his life a misery. He was also tall, tender and immensely fond of children, even ensuring that they still have half a day off from school, complete with a daffodil, on 1 March, his day.

Some in St David's believe that his qualities characterize the townsfolk, and there are almost no serious social problems here even if, when I was there, the minister in his evensong pulpit was complaining long and loud about the children who have 'no respect for man or beast'.

It has even been written that St Patrick was born here and Nona Rees claimed to have a seat in her garden on which St Patrick had sat when he had his famous vision of all Ireland. It was this vision, we were told, which encouraged St Patrick – who was really a Welshman – to sail over there and sort out the Irish. He may well, however, have had rather less success over there than St David did here.

Come the night and the cathedral looked immense and strong with its spiky outline topped by a purple, starry night. I haunted the precinct, crossing and recrossing the Penitents' Bridge which medieval pilgrims were supposed to travel over on their hands and knees. There was a chuckling stream and golden house lights hung in the darkness. 'The day is close at hand,' David said when he knew he was dying. 'I am glad to go the way of my fathers. Do the little things you have seen and heard through me.'

When news of David's impending death went out from here crowds came from all over Wales to be near him. They were about to lose their eloquent and courageous Waterman and, when he was laid to rest, even the birds struggled to control their grief.

So it is still possible to pull on – and follow – the tangled threads of history and examine the little things of a big man who was among the first to forge the template of the Celtic Heart. This was the man who taught us that darkness could not be the last word. He it was who first took a torch to the homes of the Druids and all their demons, taking us closer to the arms of a loving God and, in so doing, setting us free. This was a man of outstanding honour, virtue and passion; a man who fearlessly fought the many enemies of God while setting up standards and practices of simplicity and hard work which set the foundations of the future Welsh society.

It was a mild evening and I was standing on another bridge in the cathedral precinct when I felt a sudden blast of freezing air which made me start shivering violently. Something or someone began forming in the house lights and, despite my shivering, I noticed a beautiful blonde woman taking shape. She had the huffy hauteur characteristic of such glamorous beauty and was staring disdainfully directly at me. Her hand was holding something metallic and sharp and her coat fell apart revealing that she was as naked as the day she was born.

I blinked a lot but she disappeared, as if by the same strange trick of smoke and mirrors which had put her there in the first place. She may well, of course, have been a simple hallucination but, there again, I was sure she was something more than that. All Celts were supposed to be sensitive to the presence of evil and, first and last, I always considered myself a Celt. That strange figure may have been a hallucination but maybe she was something else again.

Perhaps the demons, with whom the old Celtic saints had once done battle so successfully, had returned. Perhaps those old agents of evil were back and busy again and, if so, the chances were high that these new demons were every bit as rapacious and evil as the old ones. I would never really know the truth so I just wandered back into the town and bought myself a bag of chips.

It was a warm, grey day late in autumn when I called into Laugharne, passing the church and a horse in a field, deep in the deepest of daydreams. A milkman was moving from door to door in a cloud of chinking bottles, and two women were standing together on the pavement in the main street outside Brown's Hotel doing what such women do the best: having a good natter.

Down the road next to the shore some rooks were flapping around a ruined castle. Further up the shoreline was a house perched on stilts and, directly above the house, in a lane, was a wooden shed, no more than a small garage, where a poet once sat at a table 'in the singing light' and produced a miraculous and glittering stream of words which barely anyone understood but flowed out through that door and astonished the world.

This was once the home of Dylan Thomas, the roaring boy on his runaway horse, whose life and work tells us much about the Celt and not all of it flattering. Dylan clearly combined some of the best and worst features of your average garrulous Celt and, if he ever got a bit chilly, while working in this shed for example, he would shout down to his wife to bring him up a few pullovers. And she would have to put them on him.

His failings were many and varied. A fat, rather ugly man, he had a Woodbine cigarette almost permanently stuck to his bee-stung lips and often a scarf curled round and round his neck like a long-dead snake. He was a colossal liar who carefully fostered the myth of a great womanizing drunk; but most of his affairs were pure fantasy and, due to a diabetic condition, he usually needed but two or three pints of beer before he fell over into a coma. His real definition of heaven was to be in a warm bath, sucking on a boiled sweet and swigging a bottle of pop, reading a trashy detective story while his wife washed his back.

When he was not writing poetry in his 'sea-shaken house on the breakneck of the rocks, high among the beaks and palavers of the birds', he was busy perfecting the art of the begging letter: a more or less continual series of agonized missives asking someone to settle this debt for him or pay for that. He often journeyed up to London broke and hoping, in some vague way, to live off women. His one universally recognized masterpiece was *Under Milk Wood*, a play for voices in which he immortalized Laugharne and created some wonderfully funny characters like the schoolmaster who was always being nagged by his wife and was, in consequence, forever planning to poison her; the girl who did it all the time because she liked babies; and the woman who every morning shouted her name to the heavens.

On the day of my visit there were already signs of an impending Christmas since the shops were announcing details of carol services, turkey darts shoots and Christmas draws. Even at midday the light was as thin as a Christmas afternoon with the river, swollen fat by the recent rain, building and reshaping the sand and mud banks on the outlying shore. Herons stood in pools and, way out on the Pendine sands, gulls wheeled above the stooped shapes of the cockle-pickers.

These sands are freedom, space and high winds. Sometimes stray shafts of sunlight pick up the cockle-pickers and their carts, making them look fiery and almost biblical.

Huge winds can come exploding in across the estuary, practically ripping the breath out of your mouth; and sometimes it can be both frightening and thrilling just being out there, bending low into the winds and fighting against them as the sand dances and whistles around your stumbling, constantly shifting feet.

I met my friend George Tremlett, a former GLC leader, with a fat genial smile, who now runs a bookshop in Laugharne. George finds the place very relaxing, giving him the peace to write his books. Yes it is indeed one of the loveliest places in Wales – almost too lovely – where you can still spot the magical, incandescent images in Dylan's work: the herons 'ankling' the pools, the incessant gabbling of the gulls, and the nearby rolling St John's Hill. Dylan said he came one day, for the day, and never left. Got off the bus and forgot to get back on again. The insanity rate in the town was so high, he also said, they had to lay on a special bus when it was visiting day in the local asylum. He had the usual Welsh penchant for exaggeration.

So finally our boyo, with his bulging eyes and mock-posh English accent, was brought back here in a coffin, dressed in a dickey bow and a smart suit, looking so unusually dapper that, when the Welsh broadcaster Wynford Vaughan Thomas and others came to look at him to pay their last respects they all burst out into laughter. Dylan had died of 'alcoholic insult to the brain' after drinking a few drinks too many in New York on 9 November 1953.

They buried him in the local cemetery where he lies beneath a plain wooden cross. The paint on the cross was flaking when I found it and the flowers were dead, with just a few plastic roses staring up out of the bedraggled mess defiantly. It seemed shocking that his grave was so badly tended, particularly as his work, thanks largely to America, is now on the verge of supporting one of the most successful and richest literary estates in the world.

In his case death really does have a rich dominion and I stood there for a while over the dead and plastic flowers, asking our Rimbaud of Cwmdonkin Drive what he made of it all but, of course, he did not reply.

Then, walking back through that Laugharne night and running many of those magical lines and phrases through my mind, I thought I understood how Dylan, like St David before him, would indeed live in the hearts and minds of the world forever. Such men manage to touch and move our secret places with their visionary splendour and they have the ability to make their own hearts sing to other hearts. Dylan's poetry always had the condition of music – he was incapable of writing a dud line – and you often found yourself profoundly and strangely moved by it, even when you could not understand a single word.

Dylan once wrote: 'Everything I write is for the love of man and in praise of God and I would be a damned fool if I didn't.' He always found the roots of faith in every landscape he ever wandered in and, like the old Celtic saints, understood the basic interconnectedness between everything there is. He also drew deeply on the Yeatsian ideal of the 'blood, imagination and intellect' all running together.

But perhaps he displayed his full Celtic colours in his love and use of words, using them like no other. The children playing in the park were 'star-gestured' and 'innocent as strawberries'. The skies were 'unminding', which is what skies always are or else he was 'singing in his chains in the sea'. A meticulous craftsman he worked and reworked his poems again and again, perhaps as many as a hundred times until they came together and, like the Psalmist, sang a brilliant new song. Predictably his favourite line in the Bible was: 'In the beginning was the Word . . .'.

Oh yes, the old poet was still here in these slumbering, cold Laugharne streets, still here in those lace curtained front parlours where the Bible was left permanently open at Revelation; still here in the golden eruptions of chatter and laughter in the front bar of Brown's Hotel; still here in the lonely, brooding chapel and those night breezes rattling the bare branches of the trees and encouraging them to give him their own round of applause.

Hush now and listen for the pounding of the old poet's heart, beating in house after house and pub after pub, beating through the far reaches of this 'Bible-black' night, beating steadily as it spins out all those words of love and praise which have saved lives – and broken them too.

The Celt was a man of deep passion and multiple failings. The Celt brought his failings to the foot of the cross and offered them up to a loving and forgiving God who understood them all too well. The Celt understood the deep secrets of praise, that act of worship, beneficial to both the worshipper and the worshipped, which is at the root of a nation's spiritual life. Dylan then, in many senses, was a Celt *par excellence*, and we know his life and work will continue to fascinate and torment us for all time.

Yet we should remember that the poet has always been venerated in almost all Celtic societies, once enjoying an authority even exceeding that of the wily old Druids. In many senses all Celts were children of poets and, even in medieval times, the best were sent to schools of poetry where they had to work through the seven grades of the poets' curriculum. A poet could actually rework landscapes and tame the most savage beast; a few well-delivered verses could even bring out blisters on the faces of your enemy. At times they became such a tiresome rabble, with their rolling rhymes and satirical wordscapes, they had to be banished and 'voided out of the realm'.

So let's at least call on the Lord to make sure our Rimbaud of Cwmdonkin Drive is comfy and warm as he lies in this damp, cold cemetery. And let's ask that one day they will at least pass round the collection plate and erect a nice tombstone on his grave and, if not that, at least bring him new prayer and fresh flowers daily, to continue giving his spirit the honour he so richly deserves.

Two nights later it was midnight dark in another Welsh town with the yellow phosphorescence of the street lamps neutralizing every other colour around them. A cat crossed the deserted road and, for a while, a shower fell on the parked cars. Raindrops gathered on the shiny bonnets in deep luminous globes which were, in their turn, loosened by the rain and sent dribbling down onto the roads and pavements.

I had come to Loughor, a town of relentless ordinariness on the bank of a river which flows out into Swansea Bay. Directly across the water were the floodlit towers of light industry and nearby was a public house called the Reverend James. The shops were closed and shuttered and a man walked past hurriedly giving me a terse but friendly 'Good night'.

Yet, impeccably ordinary though this town might be, it has long been special to me because directly across that street, in Moriah, that dark and lonely chapel surrounded by iron railings, one man stirred the conscience of this nation and began the last great Welsh religious revival with the thunder and lightning of his personality. From the very first moment I heard his story it obsessed me until, one day, I simply gave up my job in Fleet Street, handing *The Sunday Telegraph* all of ten minutes' notice and coming to live down here to begin my research into his life which finally turned into my first novel, *One Winter of the Holy Spirit*.

This man, Evan Roberts, also seemed to be another who had an instinctive grasp of the Celtic Heart and what moved it. He told the people of his tremendous visions and made them understand a holy God's requirement that his people be holy too. Without the straitjacket of any denomination he appealed to all Christians, asking for personal repentance. He also rooted his faith in an austere chapel simplicity which has always been the foundation of the Celtic Church. Quite simply he changed the mood of Wales and, in a few barnstorming months, claimed 100,000 converts. Football matches became prayer meetings, pubs closed and drunkenness dropped and, in some places like Mountain Ash, crime disappeared completely and the magistrates complained they had nothing to do.

A police panda car went past, the driver eyeing me suspiciously as I remained standing directly opposite the Moriah. It was then I noticed the lights were going on inside it and the main wooden door was half open. This seemed rather strange as I crossed the road to get closer to the door, noticing that a smartly dressed man was standing inside the vestry with a handful of hymnals.

Then, as if from nowhere, a small group of people came running out of the night, hurrying up the chapel's gravel path and disappearing into the vestry. I moved closer seeing that, far from being empty, the chapel was, in fact, packed to the rafters. I managed to shoulder my way inside and could feel my eyes shining with wonder as I stood there in a great heaving sea of people continually erupting with great waves of hymn, prayer and praise.

As these waves broke around him, in the high prow of his pulpit, Evan Roberts was standing there, hands clamped tightly together and eyes closed, deep in fervent prayer. 'This night we want the Holy Spirit to perform a great act of devastating power,' he shouted finally. 'We want this service to become one of the first repayments to God on a massive debt they now owe him. Tonight all of you are going to feel the sweet, warm breeze of Calvary on your faces.'

Evan was more than six feet tall with a pale face, hazel eyes and a large nose. His smile had the bright immediacy of fire on petrol and his right hand often gave a small and peculiar wave beneath his chin. In front of him on

70

the dais at the foot of the pulpit were his six lady singers, including the fetching Annie Davies, a small, black-eyed contralto famous for her solos, which she sang clutching a large Bible to her bosom with small head-shakings of grief.

He fell silent and there was an announcement of a conversion from the Gallery. This was followed by the singing of 'Diolch Iddo' – 'Thanks be to him for remembering the dust of the earth' – which was to become the great love song of the Revival. Also, after every conversion, the people clapped and waved so many white handkerchiefs you could be staring out over a field of newly hatched cabbage white butterflies.

It was so hot and stuffy I had to open my coat as Evan asked: 'Any one else want to confess? Anyone else wanting his life renewed and returned to him?'

An old man with short grey hair stood up, holding the Bible. 'This book of books is my chief and only guide through the brief journey of this world,' he said. 'I am now on the edge of the old river and sing in rapture at the prospect. Only the other day I had a vision of a beautiful land with the friendliest people in it. Between me and this golden country was a shining river to be crossed only by a plank. I was anxious about the crossing, fearing that the plank would not support me. But, at that moment, I gave myself to God and, on a great wave of faith, crossed to safety.'

A silence trawled through the congregation as everyone pondered on the simplicity and dignity of the man's words until Annie Davies stood up and led everyone into 'Abide with Me':

Abide with me; fast falls the eventide:
The darkness deepens; Lord, with me abide:
When other helpers fail, and comforts flee,
Help of the helpless, O abide with me.

They were about to begin the second verse when Evan

71

called out for them to stop, adding that he saw among them a man in distress. 'This man is in the struggle and about to make a decision. He is hovering on the very brink of eternal life. Step up, brother. Step into the sunlight. Receive his grace now that you may avoid his wrath. He is coming there now.'

A man's voice shouted that he had given in and the congregation began waving handkerchiefs and singing 'Diolch Iddo'.

'Another is in dire straits and about to make a decision,' Evan cried. 'His situation is too terrible for us to sing. I have never experienced such a thing before. A soul is in torment and the Lord is calling out for it. Come into the sunlight, my brother or sister. Come riding in on a wave of love.'

The heat had become as unbearable as the excitement. Almost everyone was sweating profusely. Even the lady singers, sitting safely above the throng, in their white lace blouses with leg o' mutton sleeves, were fanning themselves with their hands, their mouths sometimes opening and closing like goldfish looking for relieving oxygen on a hot, summer's day.

The bodies crushed together even more and someone behind me began praying in tongues when Evan cried out again: 'In the last days, the Bible tells us, certain things will happen. Well we are in the last days and these things are happening already ...' His lips kept moving but the words dried up. He swallowed hard and tried again. 'These things are happening already ...' The words went again when he raised his hands in horror as a believer beholding the shame of Calvary. Then the words really did come. With power. And pure fire.

'He is on his way then and will engulf the world. Satan and all his dark angels have escaped from that dungeon in hell and are even now gathering for the one last desperate rebellion against God. Beware, my people. Arm yourselves with holiness for this hurricane will tear apart

72

your lives with a terrible force. It will come enshrining the laws of Mammon which will keep you enslaved; telling of the sweetness and triumph of carnal knowledge which will destroy your family; insisting that right is wrong and that wrong is right.

'This satanic force will set up a shrine on every hearth and scatter illusions at your feet. This invading force will come as an organized and glittering intelligence. Never underestimate it since it is so clever it will come dressed as men of respectability, anxious to serve you, making you laugh and cry and even able to convince you its dark side does not exist. But it does, my people. Its dark side is pure evil and it is going to throw a cloak of violence and perversion over the face of the world.'

His head moved this way and that and his whole body vibrated like a single flower in a playful breeze. But the words were gentler now, smilingly jubilant rather than savagely apocalyptic. 'But this move to drive God from his throne will fail. Oh yes. It will fail all right. This mighty struggle between God and Satan to mount the horse of the human choice must fail in Satan's destruction. This ultimate blasphemy will end, where it began, in that dungeon in hell. But it will only fail when the powers of darkness seem to reign over the whole world; since only then, when we are weeping in our ruin, will that bruised Galilean rise again and deliver mankind in the second coming. Yes, my people, that great day when the blessed will be separated from the damned and all the dead will be resurrected in joy. Repent and prepare for the day when the Son of Man will come again in all his glory. Yes, he is coming like the sun striding down on the land but will you be ready? Are you ready if he comes tonight?' An accusing finger traced a wide arc all around. 'Well are you? Be ready. If you do nothing else at all in this life be ready for his return.'

These flaming words scorched us all and the whole chapel erupted with cries and hallelujahs. Here was

73

another man who had come before us to put on display the precious and sacred emblems of the tribe; here was another in a glittering dynasty of great preachers, a line which went right back to Hywel Dda and took in such mythic spellbinders as Daniel Rowland, Christmas Evans, William Williams and Howell Harris. Here was another one come with the thunder and all hands were raised high in salute to his vision of the coming hell. A breeze from Calvary indeed. A gale!

I turned and turned again in the cold night outside the Moriah chapel and that policeman in his panda had come back to take another look at what I was up to. A crescent moon was shining down on the lonely, empty chapel and, near the main door, was a slate obelisk marking Evan Roberts's grave. 'Here lies a man who once opened the heart of a nation', it said.

I took a few gulps of cold air knowing that somehow I had been taken by the Holy Spirit and baptized in the waters of the mighty river of Celtic life and death, full as it often is with blood, passion and pride. The Holy Spirit had given me a vision of this river's vibrance and willingness to renew itself, no matter how often and for how long it may sometimes look dried up and dead beneath bleak skies of satanic sunshine.

Bring all things to the Lord and, in my own time and my own way, I will make them new. Carry the bodies of all your loved ones to me and I will revive them in the inexhaustible spring of all my tears.

6

A Gunman on Skye

THE MACHARS OF GALLOWAY is right down on the left
hand side of Scotland, a peninsula of high winds and big
skies. On the road to Whithorn, at the peninsula tip, I
passed flat lochs and smelly piggeries. There were caravan
parks and whitewashed cottages, the odd deer on the
road and the even odder RAF jet rifling through the
skies so low it all but made me jump out of my skin. At
one point, while crossing a bridge in my camper, a jet,
which was all of six feet above me – or so it seemed –
caught me in such a loud and unwelcome clap of thunder
I thought the bridge had broken up beneath me, and I
was about to be flung straight into the river below.

There is a certain ragged beauty about this peninsula,
which is the poorest area with the highest level of unem-
ployment in Scotland, and we know the Celtic saints worshipped in these surrounding fields, setting up one of the
first monastic settlements in Europe. These open spaces
were the sites of the first great churches of the outdoors;
they were holy places where the song of birds mingled
with the song of the people; where gusting prayers were
incensed by the rain as the worshippers knelt on high,
wide altars of grass, believing that the very Spirit of God
could be seen and felt in everything that grew and moved
and flew all around them.

The town of Whithorn has long been a popular place
of pilgrimage after St Ninian founded a great monastery
here in the late fifth century. The town's coat of arms is

75

a resurgent angel, although the first I knew that I had come to a holy place was when I stopped to fill up at a garage which turned out, on closer inspection, to be an old church with a cash desk in what had been the vestry.

I followed the road further until it brought me down to an old quay with yet another petrol station, which also doubled up as a grocery store; then there was a small headland with a ruined church, a mumbling sea and a small children's playground, where two toddlers were busy walloping one another until the mother intervened, grabbed them both near the swings and angrily walloped the pair of them.

Many of the pilgrims of old would have disembarked at the quay before coming up here to this church and giving thanks for their safe arrival. Those pilgrims never knew the meaning of fear, forever jumping into small, leaky boats and sailing off into the wide, blue yonder, even getting as far as Iceland. 'Oh Lord help me because the sea is so large and my boat is so small,' said one Celtic prayer.

You can actually see five kingdoms from this headland: Scotland, England, Ireland, the Isle of Man and the Kingdom of Heaven. Further along the coast is Ninian's cave, where the old saint repaired for quiet prayer and a chat with any passing seals.

Celtic saints were forever chatting with seals and birds – and what they found to talk about all the time I do not know – but that afternoon I settled for a chat with a passing fisherman. This proved to be something of a mistake because, like an old car, once he got going he would not stop. All fishermen are nutty and this one seriously so, but some of the tips he gave me in readiness for the day when all my books are remaindered three days after their publication and I am forced to live in a cave and fish for my supper were quite interesting.

'You have to be very careful when you dig up your ragworm,' he began, 'because they have two big teeth which can give you a nasty nip. It is almost impossible to kill a conger eel, which can also give you a really awful bite, although Chinese restaurants will buy one off you if you can get it to them safely in a bucket in a reasonably passive state.' He was with a group of fishermen in a small boat when they last pulled in a conger and they all had to cling together on the top of the wheelhouse, taking it in turns to go down on the deck to try and behead the thing before finally flinging it over the side. 'The head alone will give you an awful bite.'

'There was a lot of mullet outside St Ninian's cave the other morning but two seals turned up and the whole lot took off faster than torpedoes. Mullet often will not take bait; they like to look at it and wind you up, although you can sometimes get pollack to take silver foil. Just keep shaking it from side to side like a small fish. But do watch the waves around here, because they can pick you up and carry you 200 yards out into the sea before you realize what's going on.' It helps if you are a good swimmer, which he wasn't. In fact, truth to tell, he could not swim a stroke and, when he went to the swimming baths, his wife said he swam like a plastic duck.

A few people had told me that the seven tides bring so much air into Whithorn that you often want to sleep for a fortnight and, what with the angler's many tips, of which I have given only a brief synopsis, my brain could not absorb any more information. I really did feel like sleeping for a fortnight, driving over to the nearby caravan park at Burrow Head, which was formerly a military base and prisoner of war camp, and still looks like them, as it lies scattered around a clubhouse and along a cliff.

But even in my tiredness there was a sign in the public toilet which had a certain Celtic angst about it and made me smile: WE APOLOGISE FOR THE LACK OF HAND TOWELS IN THIS FACILITY BLOCK, it said. THIS IS DUE TO SOME MINDLESS PERSONS WHO KEEP PULLING THEM OUT OF THE HOLDERS, WETTING

THEM AND THROWING THEM OVER THE WALLS
AND CEILINGS. WE CAN NO LONGER TOLERATE
THESE ACTIONS AND HAVE NO OTHER ALTERNA-
TIVE BUT TO REMOVE THE TOWELS COMPLETELY.

The next morning, after a restless, wind-buffeted night of
being attacked by fanged ragworm and bodiless heads
of congers, I went back into Whithorn to visit the old
priory there which many are now in the process of
excavating.

St Ninian built this priory in AD 450 and it became
known as Candida Casa, a sort of early mission house to
the Picts, a tribe of warrior Celts who were a constant
thorn in the sides of the Romans and who fought so furiously that the Romans called them *furor celticus*. They
looked like fierce wood demons with cloaks and long
shaggy lime-hardened hair, and whenever even their name
was dropped in Roman circles it caused immediate panic.
Before engaging in battle they sang songs and had a wide
range of 'horrible and diverse yells', beating their shields
with their swords and so determined, that they would
even stand up to their necks in water for two days if it
gave them any sort of tactical advantage. These wild
men kept the heads of their enemies pickled in cedar oil
in boxes and frequently staged raids to steal cattle. If
that did not work they would exchange their wives or
daughters for cattle. In fact the more we learn of these
early tribes who came out of the lands north of the
Alps the more miraculous it seems that they were finally
transformed into great and cultured tribes of Christian
knights. There is little of the original settlement left at
Whithorn, except the usual dislocated stone corners and
leaning piles of rubble which no one is absolutely certain
about. So far they have dug up a metalled road, evidence
of some old stake-walled structures, and the remains of a
few coffins constructed from split tree trunks.

A group of archaeologists were busy on the morning I was there, digging down into some sort of medieval cemetery with their little trowels and brushes which were revealing an unlikely sea of hip, leg and arm bones. Each archaeologist seemed to hover over his particular patch of bones as a dog might hover over his own treasured horde, now and then brushing off the centuries of dust and squinting at them with the exact care of a diamond cutter.

'This is a very good hip I've got here,' one told me with a sort of proprietorial pride. 'You'd be surprised what we can work out from bones like this. A few died from battle injuries but there is a lot of evidence of rheumatic diseases. Almost all of them died before the age of fifty and the only remaining sign of their coffins is that dark stain in the soil.'

Occasionally they found a fish hook or an old hairpin, but the early Celts believed you didn't need anything for the afterlife except perhaps a pure soul. 'Oh look there's a nice skull coming up here with a tremendous backbone down there. This belongs to someone but that head belongs to someone else again. All the toes are under here. Sometimes they just threw them in although they tended to take more care the more important the people were.'

It is always necessary to put the finds in context, another told me. Not so long ago, on another dig, they found the leg of an animal among the bones of a family. They decided the Vikings must have arrived in the middle of Sunday lunch and after slaughtering everyone tossed the whole lot into the same hole – including the Sunday lunch.

Another of the archaeologists there, Andrew Nicholson, looked a bit like a Viking with his sun glasses, cropped hair and long ponytail. He also wore a leather biker's jacket, a thick Celtic ring and Army camouflage trousers tucked into his wellies. He even liked to dress up as a

Viking in his spare time, I learned, running around fields with lots of others in those funny war games when they re-enact all the pillaging. He said he came here for a six-week holiday nine years ago and never went home again. Got off his longship and never got back on again, I thought, remembering Dylan Thomas. Came to pillage and stayed to dig.

He said he just loved digging up old bones, although how anyone can actually enjoy doing that I simply cannot imagine. I think I would even prefer to fish for conger eels than do that.

After the death of Ninian this priory became one of the largest places of pilgrimage in Europe, with thousands turning up to touch his relics. Indulgences were also sold here, and even Robert the Bruce came here one day looking for a cure for the leprosy which had plagued his later years.

The relics, indulgences and all the other fripperies of Rome were all blown away in a gale of Protestant scorn in the Reformation, but Andrew Patterson, a local minister and nationalist, who sails around these parts in a small boat called 'Captain Pugwash', and who has also been involved in setting up the Whithorn Pilgrimage Trust, says that it is almost impossible to exaggerate the importance of a monastic settlement like this. 'It was the monasticism of the Celtic Church which provided the impetus to turn Christianity from the faith of an eccentric minority into a giant force which maintained and gentled the Celtic world of the West,' he said.

It was a fine Sunday when I left the home, which is almost a small castle, of my friend Jim McFarlane; the previous night's amazing dinner was still singing hymns inside me as I followed the high road out of Glasgow and around Loch Lomond and on to Oban which, in turn, was going to take me on a ferry out to the island of Mull.

But, as I crested the high hill leading down into Oban, I began getting more and more frantic with worry since it was soon going to be three o'clock and kick-off time in the FA Charity Shield opening match of the season between Newcastle and Manchester United, which was being transmitted live on Sky television. I have long been a devoted, if not fanatical, Newcastle fan – along with my youngest son Nathan who even goes to bed in their strip – so I was doing something absolutely shameful, particularly on a journey which was supposed to be something of a holy pilgrimage searching for the soul of the Celt, and that was looking around the streets of Oban for a tell-tale satellite dish.

I spend most of my waking hours pouring scorn on – and even writing books about the evils of – television; so no one could have set about a quest more furtively or even suspiciously, peering into empty bars and cafés while also glancing behind nervously, as if I was expecting a photographer from *The Sun* to come out and snap me then put it on their front page. PILGRIM IN SATELLITE DISH SHOCKER. And it was a Sunday too!

My secret plan was to watch Newcastle, with their new record signing Alan Shearer, murder Man. U by at least six goals and then pile onto the car ferry for Mull. But it did not work out like that. I did find a bar packed with lovely Newcastle supporters, and there was a lovely television in it, but then disaster struck, since Manchester duly began dancing all over Newcastle and Alan Shearer did not seem to know his right foot from his left. The best that could be said about Newcastle was that they ran on the pitch quite well and, for the next couple of hours, all we did was keep dropping our heads into our hands and groaning in sheer disbelief at the size and scale of our hammering. By the time the final whistle blew I had also got through quite a few pints of beer – purely to relieve the pain, your honour – and ended up not going to Mull at all but spending much of the early part of the night trying to get into the wrong end of my sleeping bag in my camper in the pub car park.

The roads of Mull actually put the switch into switchback and there was certainly no snoozing at the wheel as I began negotiating the highs and the lows, the swerves and the bends of the island's single track road as it crossed tiny bridges or rode high along the side of a loch where you always had to pull in on a lay-by to let someone pass who was coming in the opposite direction. I always gave way in my camper, which was invariably greeted by a friendly wave, because I was never in a hurry to get anywhere, even if this extreme sloth often infuriated some of the motorists who built up into long queues behind me. Not that I could have picked up any real speed had I wanted. Even standing up on top of my accelerator rarely got me going faster than forty miles an hour, and that trip I had only once passed another vehicle, a lorry belching black smoke from its exhaust, which I overtook because I was going downhill and had a strong following wind.

Mull had lots of wandering, black-faced sheep either grazing on the grass or lying along the side of the road. I knew they were going to be trouble when one actually stood on the side of the road waiting for me to pass and, just as I was about to pass, he leaped head first towards my wheels like some fluffy kamikaze pilot and I only just managed to miss the bleating wretch, although I am sure I docked a good inch off his tail. There was another walking directly ahead of me – but with one eye on me – who turned away as if to let me go past but then, when I accelerated, he turned back again and tried to end it all right under my wheels.

This concept of suicidal sheep was new to me and I could not understand it. Perhaps they simply knew that they were going to end up as a pile of chops on someone's dinner plate and merely wanted to get their short and miserable lives over and done with. Certainly the sheep in my part of the world in South Wales would never countenance such a futile act; they are scabby rogues who spend their days roaming the Valley towns, erasing vegetable patches in allotments or knocking over dustbins. They will even climb on one another's backs if they think it will get them near some juicy cabbage patch, and I know a man who makes it a point of principle to always eat lamb chops in a restaurant in the hope of eating that sheep who keeps knocking over his dustbin.

But, apart from these strange sheep, Mull is something of a paradise and I could sing hymns to the island all day long. At one point I spotted a school of dolphins cruising along a loch and I pulled up to watch them. Even though they were well over 200 yards away I could clearly hear their soft snorts of air which were curiously amplified by the water and high loch wall.

There were the thrashing riffles of the salmon farms and, on one bend, an eagle broke cover from the heather, taking off with no more than two or three beats of its great wings before soaring high on a huge arc of beautiful flight.

I ended up in Fionnphort where I parked my camper and bought a ticket to the island of Iona just across the water. Some fishermen were sorting out crabs on the ferry ramp, flinging them into one box or another as the crabs, absolutely livid with the indignity of it all, did their best to snap at the fishermen's gloved hands. 'Och aye, the wee sods can even get through your gloves sometimes and give you a nasty bite.'

And there she was coming to me again – my favourite island of them all – Iona with her shops, houses and tiny slivers of white beach. Bits of sun blinked down through the clouds on the marvellous scaffolded abbey sitting there near the shoreline. In some strange but deep way I have always felt as if I am actually going home when I go to Iona; always felt that somehow my family has been entwined with this sacred place forever and that my slippers will be warming in front of the fire and my dinner in the oven as soon as I set foot on her.

They had a small new museum there and I spent some time inside, learning about life on this island which, in 1846, suffered from the potato blight when the potatoes were also destroyed throughout the West Highlands. On one day alone ninety-eight people left Iona, and it was not at all difficult for me to pick up on these terrible waves of Celtic suffering again, seeing myself sitting here and shivering with hunger in a single room, with walls of mud and a roof of dried turf. The potato beds had let us down again by going rotten and black. Clods of peat smouldered coldly in the hearth as the spectre of famine again stood, a silent and unbidden guest, in the silver light of the doorway. The real trouble with hunger is that you know it is going to last forever – even if someone does give you food, the memory of hunger will always stay with you.

I went into a small church and met a man with the most genial name of Arrick who was acting as a pilgrim guide. He was a man, you knew immediately, with whom you could talk all day long and never get bored. When I told him I was writing a book about the Celts he said there was now a Celtic web site on the Internet, maintained by an Anglican minister in Japan. Well there was nothing wrong with the Celtic spirit spreading through modern technology, we decided. Indeed the Celtica centre in Machynlleth in Wales was staging Celtic rock concerts on the Internet.

'We welcome pilgrims here who come looking for the spirit of Columba and the Celtic Church,' Arrick said. 'The Abbey here, with its emphasis on whole salvation, has echoes in Celtic theology which has always held together the spacious and the small.'

84

I learned a lot about the Celtic Christians on that visit; of how they were tremendous at stirring people to faith, always offering society a model of stability even in times of spiritual collapse. They were also inspired story-tellers rather than dry theologians, borrowing the best of the old beliefs and putting their own stamp on them. Their one outstanding gift was the life of the imagination and, as it evolved, the Celtic faith was a means of connecting with God and with every aspect of life which had spiritual significance. Their sympathy was always with the underdog.

The Celtic belief, I was also told that day, does not have the ethereal spirituality of the New Agers with their stars, moons and ley lines. The Celtic belief is a thing of the senses, based on the natural world and all that is fine in that world.

A flock of wild geese, for example, one of the earliest symbols of the Holy Spirit in the Celtic Church, has a 70 per cent greater range than a lone goose. An arrowhead of geese, with each individual taking it in turns to become the front flier, who has to work much harder than the rest, until he tires, can also fly 75 per cent faster. Any Church which celebrates such a co-operative effort by using them as a symbol of the mighty arm of God has a nice eye for their functional practicality. Geese are also faithful and pair for life; they look after their young diligently and mourn the loss of their mate.

Later I met a fellow Welshman, Dafydd Owen, the director of the MacLeod Centre. The centre takes youngsters from such unpromising places as the slums of Glasgow, and gives them a week of fun and the arts. Some are former drug addicts or petty criminals but no one is excluded. Dafydd added that the young seem to have an instinctive understanding of – and feeling for – the Celtic religion. 'They like its sense of justice and thought for the dispossessed. There's no airy fairyness or

smells and bells here. This is a faith which has social rel-
evance and actually works. It sticks up for young people
like them.'

It was becoming dark when I walked up to the abbey
ruins and the Street of the Dead, a graveyard where sixty-
four kings from Macbeth to King Duncan lie buried.
John Smith, the former Labour leader, lies here beneath
this watchful Hebridean twilight and I paid my respects
to his grave which has a smooth grey granite slab on it.
'An honest man is the noblest work of God' it said in
gold lettering on the slab, and I put a small pebble there
to go with the others.

A cold breeze picked up and kept quivering in the
buttercup meadows like grief. Sheep looked at me as I
wandered down to that rocky, holy shoreline, reminding
me of my Welsh home. But I had to keep telling myself this
place was, in a sense, home since it would have been
somewhere around here, somewhere along this very
shore, that Columba had arrived in 563, with just twelve
disciples, after a battle in Ireland in which 3,000 died. He
had come, he said, determined to convert as many to
Christ as had died in that battle. He did far more than
that. He built an abbey and a centre of learning. He planted crops and sent out his brilliant students who, in turn,
evangelized all the other warring Celtic tribes, instilling
in them a love of scholarship, music and song. He first
gave us all our faith.

And so it was that, with a strange music in my heart,
I stood on the shore looking at the strange drifts of light
and shadow in that dying day, staring out at the sea and
trying to see right into the start of things. I had particularly liked the line that the Celtic Church gave the life of
the imagination and it was then that I saw a small rowing
boat coming across the water towards me with one man
pulling on the oars. This man, however, was like no other
since he seemed to be enshrouded in a brilliant white
light.

I felt no fear as I turned to walk with the spirit of Columba back to the abbey where we could hear lots of those Glaswegian youngsters shrieking at one another near the gate to the cemetery. I could not even get an exact sense of what my new companion looked like beneath his veil of white light but, if my presence bothered him, he did not show it as I tagged along in his wake like a devoted dog.

We passed the shrieking youngsters and moved into a deep darkness when a white horse which seemed to be mysteriously infused with the same white light came trotting towards us. My man put both his arms around the horse's neck and began talking softly into its ears which kept twitching attentively. Every so often the horse's head bent low in submission; then something strange happened: the horse began to moan piteously with huge tears pouring out of its eyes. The man began talking into its ears again but the more he spoke the more unhappy the horse became, now wailing out loud in the most bitter lament.

He finally left the horse and walked on to bless the granary and the animals in their pounds and the stone monastery itself which had taken so much time to build. The monks kept coming out of the darkness and knelt in front of him with heads bowed. He blessed each and every one of them in turn.

By now all the monks had come out of the darkness to be with him, each of them holding a tallow candle as he walked up a small hill and blessed the whole island with upraised arms. 'Iona of my heart, Iona of my love. Even if the world will come to an end Iona will always stay as it was.'

Huge and brilliant wings began beating their way through the night from the direction of Mull – seven, ten, maybe twenty pairs of them – all now adding to the magical and holy lustre of this amazing Hebridean evening. The man lowered his arms and bowed as the

87

angels circled above his head like so many golden vultures. Handfuls of diamonds were being scattered every-which-way and the music of this sky was astonishing in its beauty and strangeness.

Columba descended the hillock and walked slowly and painfully to the church which again filled with the most luminous and yet forlorn light as he entered. There were many nervous groans and expectant sighs as we crowded around the main door when the light disappeared. Others brought more tallow candles of their own as we moved closer together with the warm breath of one another on our cheeks. A few went into the church darkness followed by a few more. Faces of anxious angels kept appearing at open windows. I managed to get inside but none of us moved or even spoke as we looked down on the body of our beautiful, brave leader as he lay there stretched out before the altar with a lone dove standing on his chest.

The weeping began, softly at first, but building up with power until my man's eyes opened and his whole face was suddenly alive with cheerfulness. Then, with another benediction for us all, he died and we cried out our pain, moving forward with raised palms and shouting 'No, no, no.'

Many stayed with him but many more of us finally moved out into that weeping night until a wind began roaring in over the sea and a huge pillar of fire started to build up over Mull, even lighting up parts of Ireland. The wind turned into a tempest within minutes, ripping the tips off the waves which, in their turn, became so high and rough for three days that no mourners could get over here from Mull. As soon as the funeral took place, the 'tempest fell, the wind ceased and the whole ocean became quite calm.' The angels had taken my man of light home.

I left Iona and managed to get off Mull a few days later without killing any depressed or suicidal sheep, taking the tiny ferry out of Tobermory and crossing over to Kilchoan on the Scottish mainland. I have to say little had prepared me for the next leg of my Celtic pilgrimage up the west coast to Skye, because I began moving through one of the most seductive and inspiring landscapes that I have ever seen, let alone travelled through.

Take the mountains of Snowdonia in Wales and mix them thoroughly with the lakes in England's Lake District. Chuck in a few of the smaller Himalayan ranges and sprinkle liberally with a few energetic waterfalls. Next take a lone bagpipe player and place carefully in the middle of the lot and dampen it all with a giant watering can which will simulate lots and lots of rain. Throw in the tiniest – and I mean tiniest – slices of sunshine and you will be coming close to what it is like around here; an unbelievable, mountainous waterworld where sea sucks on the jagged mouths of open rock and all manner of birds glide high and then tumble and fall as the very skies are engaged in vast and often noisy shunts of light and rain, with black clouds turning into wet, sunny mist and then back again, sunsets starting well enough but then running out of puff, and sunrises rising with a spritely and determined vigour only to change their minds and go hiding behind the skirts of yet more mist.

You keep turning one bend, thinking, well, that last bit was amazing, when you drive into another bit which is even more amazing. At one stage I felt I was being injected by all this ruined beauty and even had the sensation that a frozen shoulder, which had been bothering me for ages, was actually being cured by these continual injections of beauty except that, when I returned to Wales, the anaesthetic had clearly worn off and my shoulder managed to refreeze itself.

Such a landscape can play little tricks on you though, as when I spotted a lovely cairn of free-standing rocks and I had to stop to take a closer look, only to discover that they had not been built in some holy and subtle symmetry but had, in fact, been piled high on top of an old bra and a dirty pair of underpants, complete with a few decorative sprays of heather, the complex symbolism of which escaped me completely.

My next stop was Loch Shiel where Bonnie Prince Charlie rallied his troops to start the Jacobite rising in 1745. But I was not interested in Charlie so much as the old Celtic saint Finian who, according to my Ordnance Survey map, once had his own private chapel on the other side of the loch. Things were looking extremely promising here because not only had I managed to find an empty field next to the loch in which to stay overnight – with the exception of a family of bee-keepers in the far corner – but I also managed to hire a small motor launch quite cheaply which would take me across to this chapel and give me a chance to sniff around in the old saint's life and times.

There is nothing sweeter than when a pilgrimage is going well and I was feeling very smug indeed as I braked my camper next to the loch, taking a fat steak out of my fridge and slapping it on my grill and cracking open a bottle of fine wine which I set out on my little table complete with a knife and fork and a napkin. Also it was not raining – or even threatening to. The sun was about to settle down behind that mountain in a furious rage of primary colours. Ah me, this really was the life and no mucking about.

The steak cooked marvellously and actually dissolved in my mouth after barely the hint of a chew. My first sip of wine promised raptures without end too. After sitting down on my chair and offering up a quiet prayer of thanks, I lifted knife and fork, spreadeagled my elbows wide and was about to tuck in when I felt a slight tickling on the end of my nose, and on my cheeks and in my hair and all over my arms . . . There they were, floating about in my wine and all over my steak; oh blimey, I'd read about these often enough and here they were, millions and millions of them, the famous, dreaded midges of the Highlands who look like the tiniest moths, gathering here with the express purpose of biting me all over, pinching my wine and ruining my supper which they managed in about that order.

Now it felt as if about six of them were figure-skating on my bald patch or else trying to tie knots in my eyelashes or even pot-holing up my nostrils and I had to dive into the back of my camper, slam the door behind me and splatter the ones who had chased me inside with a spray – and getting most of them too – before looking sadly out at my little table with its wine and steak sitting there beneath a dense floating cloud of the little sods who between them and the rain had all but killed off the Scottish tourist industry.

Let's get one thing straight before we proceed. There is no Celtic nonsense about the sacred interconnectedness between all things when it comes to Highland midges. They are not in the holy scheme of things; they are a vast mistake who deserve only a good squirt from a really deadly spray. The deadlier the better. And it only then occurred to me that those were not bee-keepers on the other side of the field at all but some crazy family – probably English – who were wearing midge hats.

The midges were waiting for me to come out the next morning but I fooled them and did not even take the boat I had paid for, anxious to put as many miles as possible between this doomed field and me. All I did was drive over to the bee-keepers, who were indeed English, and told them, after lowering my window for a fraction of an inch, that, as I had paid for the boat they could have it for the day if they wanted. Me, I was out of here with no plans whatsoever to return.

Perhaps it was those midges and perhaps I was starting to get homesick and perhaps it was something I ate but my peace of mind began unravelling pretty swiftly after I took the car ferry from Mallaig over to Armadale on the Sleat peninsula of the Isle of Skye.

Here was one lone pilgrim who had run out of pilgrim puff, not especially roused by the extraordinary patchwork of high mountain and wild bog all around him and, in fact, especially depressed by the density of the traffic and the coaches and crowds of tourists, many sporting American accents and – my current irritation – baseball caps worn back to front. It would have been something to have been able to lie in the sun for the day to relax and recharge but there was still no sign of the sun and an almost permanent promise of yet more rain.

I simply did not feel like doing any work, which was a shame since Skye has been thought of as one of the most important centres for Gaelic cultures in Europe and has also been associated with a long list of Celtic heroes and heroines like Scathan, a famous woman warrior and the mighty Cuchulain, who learned about love and war here.

But I could not get going somehow, visiting the Clan Donald Visitor Centre, which I had been told was good, but which I found predictable and boring. These centres seem to believe that, if you put the whole story, complete with a few ancient fuzzy maps, on video, the exhibition becomes exciting and innovative. I reckon that excitement and innovation is *not* to put something on video. And anyway we are all fed up to the back teeth with television. The shop there was full of expensive tartan kitsch and the sound of bagpipes kept wheezing out of every loudspeaker. And those midges were around too.

So I was in a strange, fretful mood in the town of Broadford when I saw someone walking down the main street along the bay who may – or may not – have been there. First there was a small party of school children pouring out of the tourist office and then, behind them, was a tall, muscular and sly man wearing just a strip of tatty cloth around his midriff and two bandoliers of ammunition criss-crossing his chest. He was carrying an automatic rifle in one hand and, as he walked past me, he just glared at me hard with wide, black eyes set in a ruggedly handsome face.

And then he was gone.

Later I drove out to the Cuillin mountain range, planning to spend some time there, parked near a youth hostel and walked along a stone path for a while. These peaks are among the most dramatic anywhere, poking up out of the surrounding mists, and I was thinking I might try and climb one of them when the man with the automatic rifle appeared again in a celluloid vision on the side of the mountain some hundred yards away. Every part of his body positively rippled with muscles as he raised his gun aloft and shouted in a voice which must have carried right up the mountain: 'I have found another willing servant in Dunblane, and my mission in the world is far from finished . . .'

He disappeared and the shock of seeing him made me throw up on the path, my belly just heaving with pure acid again and again. Right, that was enough for now and, stopping only for petrol, I hopped in my camper and rattled all the long way home to South Wales.

7

The Dogs of the Liffey

—◁▷—

ONCE PAST CLONDALKIN the land became dusty with dereliction and I knew that Dublin was not far away. The ground was stained with oil and littered with bright shards of glass. Dogs in barbed wire compounds growled at me. Ragged strips of plastic had caught in the teeth of the wire, flapping in the breeze like lines of bait waiting to entice passing plastic fish. Rusty and burned-out cars lay scattered about, their motoring days at an end.

Over on the other side of the canal were the old Guinness filter beds, once used to slake the thirst of a thirsty world and now empty and covered over with weeds. A kingfisher looked at me and darted up the canal path. A lot of people have drunk a lot of water from these parts one way and another. Dubliners actually drank this water, untreated, until the end of the last century. Guinness used millions of gallons of the stuff here and it was also widespread practice for the canal men to tap off the barrels for their own use, more often than not ending up drunk on these banks. When the company changed from wood to metal barrels the canal men found their way into those too and siphoned off 'the foaming ebon ale'. Maybe it did them good. A Guinness a day and all that.

It might barely seem possible but the canal path to Dublin got dirtier and grubbier. Huge council estates with satellite dishes on the back walls of the houses sprawled around. Children were playing in bare school yards. Lots of inhabited houses near the canal had boarded-up windows with broken bottles stuck in cement on the tops of garden walls. All had burglar alarms and yet more dogs, tethered on long lengths of rope, barking and growling at me. This has become a lawless society.

The rhythms of the city became more intense. The traffic was thicker with gaudy advertisements tacked on the end of fortified terraces. Modern office blocks crowded in on the canal itself. These trees along the canal once cost three shillings and six pence each, I learned in a guide book, planted so that they would be 'a pleasing recreation as well as a salutory walk to the inhabitants of Dublin'. Thick cloud moved in over the city and it speckled with cold rain.

Directly ahead of me a figure was sitting on a bench. There was something wrong with him but I could not quite work out what it was. He had an astonishing static quality about him with one leg sticking straight out and a hat perched precariously on the back of his head. I walked forward carefully, only to discover that the figure was, in fact, a cast-iron statue of Patrick Kavanagh, the sublime wordsmith from Monaghan, iron trilby on his head and iron newspaper in his pocket, with raindrops chasing one another off the tip of his iron nose and gathering in a little puddle in his iron lap. 'Leafy-with-love banks and the green waters of the canal, posing redemption for me', it said on his plaque.

Green-headed mallard cruised the canal looking for something to eat as fat rain drops dartboarded the water all around them. The afternoon light was failing fast but I was determined to walk into the centre of Dublin before dark, crossing busy road after busy road yet still sticking to the canal until it brought me down to yet another deserted dockland area with acres of empty, grey water; abandoned warehouses and cobbled streets told of yet another thrumming era when, both as the start of the Grand Canal and the main trading artery in and out of the city, these parts would have been alive with the screech of pulleys and creak of cranes as the tradesmen with their ledgers and dockers with their hooks went about their ceaseless business.

But not any more they weren't. There was no life or commerce here as I walked under a stone archway which brought me down to Sir John Rogerson's Quay with the giant drum of its resident gasometer and the sniffy Liffey. Directly behind me were the two huge chimneys of Poolbeg, painted in red and white circles, buoyantly in contrast to the grey, belching industry they serviced. I paused next to a moored naval patrol boat.

So here she was again, this dirty old town, for my money the capital city of all the Celts, rising up on the smelly river in this thickening twilight. Up there was O'Connell Street Bridge and, further on again, the black silhouette of the Victorian ironwork of the Ha'penny Bridge. The hum of the early evening traffic rose and fell in the rain.

Then I came across a shrine which was not a shrine, since every corner of Windmill Lane was covered in coloured swathes of graffiti all in praise of the pop group U2: *Carol was there and now I'm here*; *We'll follow you to the end of the world*; *I was a sailor, I was at sea, I was under the waves before U2 rescued me*; *U2 you show us colours when there's none to see*; *U2 I can't live without you*.

This is their recording studio and I have met Bono the singer and listened to a number of their gigs. U2 are first and last a Celtic band who perform with a raw-edged and blinding, heart attack passion although, on studying the graffiti a bit more, I was amused to find one further line: *U2 are crap*. Yes, in every assembly there is indeed always one heretic.

I continued walking on up into the city past a man in a shabby raincoat shouting the truth of his madness. Even in the rain women with babies in large shawls were holding out boxes and begging. There were piles of litter and drifts of orange peel and scrunched-up tin cans – all somehow in character with the Gothic seediness of the place which probably looked as though it was about to fall down when it was first built. I passed a giant anchor put there to commemorate the seamen who had died while serving on Irish merchant ships. The tide had gone out with vertical and strangely symmetrical pendants of curling seaweed hanging off the quay walls. A shop was called Abrekebabra and there was the Dublin Barber Shop and another called the Mortgage Shop. An old television set rested on its side on the Liffey mud. The smell of the river was the same as ever; not so much one stench as a whole gang of quarrelling stenches which came together to form one memorable and abiding pong. Further up again was the main railway bridge advertising Carlsberg Lager and Irish Permanent.

The new Talbot Memorial Bridge came next, together with a statue of Matt himself put up by the Dublin Matt Talbot memorial committee. Dublin could once have been floated on a sea of alcohol and many areas in Matt's time were little more than giant shebeens with 16,000 arrests for drunkenness in 1865 alone. Even by 1900 some 9,000 people a year were being charged with being drunk and disorderly while this same city uses about thirty adjectives for being drunk, ranging from being plastered to legless or langers or stocious. Matt was as bad as any of them until he received a vision when he was standing on this bridge and about to throw himself into the water. There was a shining light and a voice said, 'Matt, Matt why are you hurting yourself in this way? Matt, Matt the time has come for you to be born again.'

And Matt was born again, giving up the black stuff for good and becoming a founder member of the Pioneer Total Abstinence Association, a sort of early Celtic AA. There are moves to canonize him, truly making him the patron saint of alcoholics. But it will probably take a long time to get through all the paperwork on that one.

I crossed over O'Connell Street Bridge and came to Ha'Penny Bridge, built in 1865 and taking its name from the old toll. I have been coming back to this bridge for almost thirty years – once coming here with the novelist Edna O'Brien who was launching a book and ending up in a party which was so drunken I got on the wrong plane home. It has always been something of a private game of mine to stand on this bridge with my hands holding on to the railings and feeling the thump of passing footsteps in my own feet. Here I try and listen to the heartbeat of Dublin and check on her general health.

But the patient wasn't too hot these days, I diagnosed, and I couldn't find any regularity in her heartbeats. In fact I was getting the strong impression that she had gone on the blink, unable to decide whether she wanted to be a goody or a baddy as she sat up in her mental ward with a contraceptive in one hand and a rosary in the other. There were lots of intimations of violence and crime in this hospital ward with many of the nurses secretly drug-addicted and a few priests down on their knees praying for the recovery of the patient's health. A lot more had given up on the practice of prayer altogether.

The sun finally sank behind a skyline of green glass office blocks and broken-necked cranes. Every now and then came the long hiss of a lorry's brakes. The city and office workers were still hurrying past me, heads down and determined to get home fast, taking no notice of the man at the rail and looking up the river. I was another bit part player on the giant sprawling stage of Dublin's street theatre.

At that moment the patient on her bed groaned out loud before screaming for help and my hands gripped that railing so hard I might have been in danger of leaving my palm prints on it permanently.

Freezing cold gusts of air began moaning up out of the side streets. A huge lazy flash of light curled through the sky which became so bright it made me squint. And there it was . . . a huge fireball rolling up the Liffey and heading directly towards me. Whole bridges were cracking with the heat of this fireball which seemed to be both widening and flattening as it made the whole city rise up on a massive bed of volcanic fire.

The fireball held the shapes of the distant railway bridges and surrounding buildings within its glow but there were other alien beings moving around inside it. There were motorcyclists wearing sun glasses and carrying shotguns. I saw cars accelerating this way and that until one went crashing into a shop window. There was the unmistakable rat-a-tat-tat of a Thompson machine gun, the shadows of people falling dead. A pack of savage dogs came running down from the roof of the sky towards me, about twenty of them and by far and away the scabbiest dogs I have ever seen, many with ripped ears and their ribs sticking out of their filthy coats. Long driblets of sputum hung out of their slavering mouths and they occasionally fought among themselves, snarling frenziedly as they bit one another and rolled this way and that. Way above the dogs, high and deep inside the inferno, several dark angels flew slowly through the Dublin night.

The sweep of all this fiery movement was being staged to the savage and continual music of riot, all coming towards me and threatening to engulf me too. That was the worst part. It was all threatening to destroy me. Me! I decided I had better make a run for it, knocking some of the homebound office workers out of the way as I dashed off the Ha'Penny Bridge and crossed the road, still hearing the roar of destructive fire in my ears as I raced through a courtyard frantically searching for something – anything at all – which would give me shelter from all those dogs and fire.

I ran along the fire-flashed pavements of Edward

Dame Street which brought me up to Trinity. The fireball was continuing to roar through the skies above my head, making the library and college glow as if they were inside a steel furnace. Those motorcyclists were still whizzing through the fire and more gunshots rang out as yet another car smashed into a window. Another pack of slavering, barking dogs went streaming through the skies but at least the sounds of riot had died away except for those siren gusts of freezing air which were still moaning around every corner.

The skies cleared again when I came to Grafton Street pedestrian precinct, passing a statue of Molly Malone with her wheelbarrow and moving on up through the glitter of the shop fronts and neon signs where punks were standing in bored groups and the odd buskers were serenading passers-by in the doorways of shops such as Saxone, Switzers and The Body Shop. The strong smell of coffee came from Bewley's Oriental Café.

The firestorms had gone, leaving me feeling desperately stiff and cold so I decided that AA or not and Matt Talbot or not I simply had to have one, if not several, stiff drinks, hanging a right into Harry Street, stumbling over some drifts of dead flowers and going into McDaids pub where I could enfold myself in the Guinness shadows of a corner.

The bar was crowded with the usual bunch of alcoholics and yarners, all busy talking as they threw down drink after drink. 'Yer man went missing for a few days and found himself under a bed in Ballybunion. What he couldn't work out was who had shaved him.' McDaids has long been a regular hangout for Dublin writers and the gossip was that the old man in the far corner had been writing the same magnum opus for the last forty years and he had not got on to the second chapter yet.

Brendan Behan, Flann O'Brien, Patrick Kavanagh and the 'Pope' Mahoney all fell over in here at some or another. They pretended to love one another but there was nothing but a fund of jealousy and hatred between them, and a Dublin literary movement was once described as a dozen writers who hated one another wholeheartedly. Patrick Kavanagh used to sit at that stool trying to find just 'wan stinking word' to finish a poem, while Flann O'Brien was a great favourite in the bar too. One of Flann's novels had two men in aqualungs chatting with St Augustine in an underwater cave off Dalkey.

What we find in this kind of writing, perhaps, is the usual Celtic difficulty with reality: the way the Celt likes to cloak the real world with fantasies and visions and his preparedness to seek out the secrets and meanings of life with a sort of visionary intensity and imaginative power. It is probably wise not to trust a single one of them.

Yet Irish writers had an unparalleled importance in the creation of modern Ireland. With their relentless energy and thrilling passion they created a nationalist revival after their art produced a massive period of self-examination. They set up a dynamic reaction between the slumbering Celts and the overweening power of the English; they enabled a fallen race to stand on their own two feet and announce they were no longer prepared to step forward and guzzle the English colonialist swill. It is amazing what can happen to a people when they get together and say 'No'. They were not going to put up with this any more, they announced, and they were going to say 'No'. And in so doing their writers enabled them to rediscover the passion and pride of their real Celtic roots; their writers really did make this country just as the Scottish ones are now doing. It is a shame that the Welsh are not doing the same.

This city has produced some of the greatest Celtic wordsmiths in W. B. Yeats, Oscar Wilde, Bernard Shaw,

Sam Beckett and Seamus Heaney. And who better or more memorably charted the vast and extravagant longings of the Celtic Heart than W. B. Yeats? But on the issue of the greatest Celtic writer I would unhesitatingly plump for James Joyce, that huge, blind god, full of uncompromising majesty and wordy power, whose spirit still broods and composes in the many pubs and snugs of Dublin.

Joyce was no fan of the priests whom he often comically blamed for the miseries of Ireland. Neither did he like Dublin, which he described as a 'centre of paralysis', but, almost alone of all the Irish writers, he staked out his art clearly in the real world with real situations and real people. He said of his epic *Ulysses* that, if Dublin were to be destroyed, the city could be recreated using his book as a site map. His was a search for the 'random, the commonplace, the ordinary' which he invested with a mythic and visionary power. He was looking for the 'irreducible modalities of the visible' and, in Bloom's and Daedelus's journeys through a day in the life of Dublin, we see again and again a real writer recreating a real world and then transforming it into art. With his pen Joyce created a new urban language and enabled Dublin to experience a mythic rebirth. Vivid and inspired, he became the godfather of all the poets and writers who have since thronged these seedy bars and streets 'setting the imagination in search of the fabulous word'. For this search really was Celtic and intensely religious. Joyce's pen affirmed each and every Dubliner's divinity; his right to be free and choose to live under the sovereign rule of God.

Mind you, it has long been a strong personal theory of mine that anyone living and growing up in 'me jewel an' darlin' Dublin has a better chance here than anywhere of becoming a writer if only because of being surrounded by the most astounding characters. One man's name was Love, Joy and Peace, so-called because that's what he inscribed on the walls everywhere; President Keely who made loopy speeches around St Stephen's Green – 'The sun will never go down on Dublin; it will do exactly as I say'; and Johnny Fortycoats who used to like wearing three or four coats no matter if it was winter or summer.

But my favourite was Bang Bang, alias Lord Dudley, who used to move around the Dublin pavements toting a silver key and shouting 'Bang, bang. You're dead.' He terrorized whole areas – buses, cinemas, anyone out walking their dog. Grown men dived for cover and old ladies ran the other way when he was abroad in the street holding that deadly key. After Bang Bang was forced to retire from gunslinging because of his failing eyesight they put him in a home for the blind run by the Rosminian Order in Drumcondra, and it was there in his later years that I sat with him for a while one afternoon next to his bed.

He was a delightful man with stooped shoulders and an Adolf Hitler hair-do, his eyes the milky-grey colour of the blind. He asked to take my hand. 'Your hand sir. It's so soft and warm. But they've got me now sir. Caught me unawares they did, unawares. I shot them all in my time. I showed no mercy and never missed. The city was mine.' He produced two large silver keys from his pocket. 'These were my 45s sir. The people tried to get away from me but they couldn't. They were never fast enough. But Dublin misses me sir. The people miss me. I want to go back and clean the place up for them but it's the eyes. I only see shadows now sir. But your hand. It really is so warm.'

When I left him he lifted up his walking stick and took aim. 'Bang, bang. You see sir? You're dead. Didn't know did you? I may not be able to use my 45s any longer but this is my rifle now and that never misses either.'

Bang Bang died a few years back although he remained an amusing oddball right up to the end, even writing to newspapers and complaining when they called him Bang

Bang rather than his preferred title of Lord Dudley. Thousands, including the Lord Mayor, turned up the day he was buried in what was almost a state funeral. Almost everyone there knew one thing: that a part of their Dublin youth and life had gone forever.

I was over in Stephen's Green the next day, looking at the gaunt iron figures of the famine in the park, when I felt reality dissembling again and, for a moment, that famine came back to haunt me; I found myself standing in a line of exhausted, ragged people in this park, all waiting for our thin gruel of Indian maize. The queue was orderly and silent. It was that deathly silence that was always the hardest to take . . . and there was . . .

The hallucination stopped soon enough but I did then jump into a taxi and went over to the National Botanical Gardens in the suburb of Glasnevin; a place which takes us to the very heart of the Celtic experience and much of her suffering.

The gardens themselves sprawl over many acres and some of those yews were planted here early in the eighteenth century, while that cedar on the other side of the Rock Garden is more than a hundred years old. This is a handkerchief tree from China and over here is a Caucasian elm. Even at this wintry time of the year you could see the bloom on those tassel bushes from California, not forgetting the mesmerizing scents from the honeysuckle and witch hazel.

Directly adjoining these gardens is Glasnevin cemetery – a really good cemetery as cemeteries go, the largest in the Republic and the only one with its own crematorium. The superintendent once took me on an engrossing tour along its many avenues and past all the clock-faced Celtic crosses. All the great Irish movers and shakers are down in here somewhere. Eamon de Valera was over there as was Charles Parnell. Gerald Manley Hopkins was under that fat boulder on the Jesuit plot and here was Michael Collins. Brendan Behan, mercifully silent at last, lay in the IRA plot. They were renovating the tomb of Daniel O'Connell – the Great Liberator – on the day I was there and I was taken down into the crypt where I was able to smooth my hand along the thick polished wood of his coffin. This hand of mine had also once held the hand of Bang Bang's, I thought inanely, so it might even now have a place and meaning in Irish history if only I could wrap my brain around it.

O'Connell's coffin had a splendid position in the middle of the crypt, though his wife and children had been put out of the way and looked like a stray pile of discarded bookshelves in some little ante-room, which seemed a bit unfair.

But the Botanical Gardens here are important to my narrative – yes, there is a narrative – because of one man, David Moore, a former curator, who not only did some interesting botanical work by germinating orchids from seeds for the first time, but also investigated the causes of the failure of the potato crop which led to the disastrous famine years.

Moore battled it out for days and weeks on end in that house, trying to find a solution to the potato blight in what became a sort of botanical detective story, one of the longest games of hide and seek in natural history. But he cracked the problem of *phytophthora infestans* and how different everything might have been if the world had listened to him. It is even possible that a million souls might not have perished had they listened to him. But they did not.

The worst outbreak of the blight appeared in Ireland in 1845 when the potato fields blackened overnight. The fields had suffered from drought in the past but nothing as destructive as this. The blight was as pervasive as frost and spread with the speed of cholera. All anyone knew for certain was that a black spot had appeared on a leaf then spread throughout the plant, destroying its life forms and making it suffer from a kind of dropsy.

Almost every potato plant went down with it and the best guesses were that it had something to do with the unusual weather that summer. It had been a hot July followed by three weeks of torrential rain and fog. No one knew anything for certain but, as usual, this did not inhibit anyone and there were any number of wild theories. The letters columns of most newspapers kept bubbling with some new speculation or other. Some blamed the smoke from the 'new' locomotives and others said it was caused by the vapours from 'blind' volcanoes or even discharges of electricity. The merely daft put it down to the hand of God.

You name it and they tried it. Potatoes were dried in lime, had salt spread over them, and were even treated with chlorine gas. But nothing worked for the simple reason that no one had the smallest clue what had caused the blight. No one knew if the blight came from the earth, water, heaven or even, as seemed more likely, hell. And without this basic knowledge they could not stop it.

Enter David Moore at Glasnevin who began collecting the rotten potato tubers from all parts of Ireland and examined them. All that could be seen with the naked eye was a white fringe of down which, it soon became clear, was a new type of fungus. The microscope revealed that the fungus itself was a complex creation of filaments and millions of spores.

But did this fungus cause the blight or was it merely an effect?

Moore gradually unlocked the secrets of this fungus, such as that it was aquatic at some time in its existence. It needed at least some water for its many spores to form and multiply, which is why it always seemed to do so well after periods of heavy rain. But how then did the spores travel? Was it on the wind? But, if so, how did they manage to get down into the earth and attack the deepest-lying potatoes? The fungus did not seem to have a root system. It only looked half complete. Where were its sexual organs? Was it hermaphroditic?

Slowly Moore unveiled the miscellaneous principles of evil which the fungus represented but, incredibly, the world did not listen to him. The conventional wisdom was that the fungus was a saprophyte, a plant that lived on the dead. It simply could not attack flourishing foliage or establish itself on a healthy host which would fight it with its own internal life forces. The decomposition had to come first; the plant was already decaying when the fungus formed.

As the powers that be clung to the belief that the fungus was a consequence of the blight and not the cause, so the blight continued to rage untreated and there was more suffering in Ireland than at any time in her history. The misunderstanding stood at the centre of a botanical gridlock which took a further forty years to unsnarl, by which time a further million had died and the country was flat on her back.

Dean Swift had been Ireland's most influential writer particularly with the satiric savagery of his *Modest Proposal*, in which he had suggested that the eating of pauper infants might alleviate the excesses of an earlier famine. 'As to this country, there have been three terrible years' dearth of corn and every place strowed with beggars,' he wrote to Alexander Pope. 'Imagine a nation the two-thirds of whose revenues are spent out of it, and who are not permitted to trade with the other third, and where the pride of women will not suffer them to wear their own manufactures even where they excel what comes from abroad. This is the true state of Ireland in very few words. These evils operate more every day, and the kingdom is absolutely undone, as I have been telling it often in print for these ten years past.'

When Swift died he left all his money to establish a lunatic asylum in Dublin. 'No nation needed it more.'

The village of Slane looked unremarkable when I got there later that week with rough-cut stone houses scattered around the main crossroads. People were milling about in the Conyngham Arms in their best finery ready for a wedding. There were a few shops to meet the needs of the 700-odd population, some iron lamp standards in the main street, and a huge Gothic stone gate which used to be the start of the drive to the castle but isn't any more, which is just as well because the castle had been burned down and is now awaiting a vast sum of money to restore it.

But the main feature of Slane, and one which draws all eyes to it, is the hill which towers over the rooftops and looks out over the Boyne valley with its winding river. I puffed up that hill finding a small ruined abbey up there with a frozen jumble of Celtic crosses in the graveyard. Up on this hill, on a clear day like this, you could see almost everything for about 120 miles, including the boats sailing into Drogheda, the lumpy masses of the Wicklow and Dublin mountains, the conical peak of the Sugar Loaf and, to the north-east, the Colley peninsula and, behind that again, the Mountains of Morne.

As it is today, so it was when I first came here as one of St Patrick's camp followers – a low, matted kingdom of mountain, river and buttercup dale in which almost nothing has changed in any real detail except, perhaps, for the chimneys of that new cement factory over in Platin.

Patrick chose this hill of Slane because it was instantly visible from that distant peak over there, some nine miles away as the crow flies: the hill of Tara, once the cultural and political capital of Ireland where kings reigned long before the first Roman set up his camp on the Tiber. Tara was also known as the Hill of Supremacy, since whoever ruled it also ruled Ireland, and therefore Patrick knew that he had to claim it in the name of God. And so it was that we built a huge paschal fire right on this spot on the hill of Slane, with which we warned King Laoghaire, the High King, that his days of glory were numbered and that a long reign of Druidic evil and pestilential demons was over.

Back in the fifth century fire was about power and territory. Victims were burned as sacrifices and, at such times, all other fires had to be put out. Only the king himself could light the first and main fire, which endowed him with jurisdiction over his territory. Other men had to kindle their own fire from the king's fire and, for each kindling, he received a tax of one screaball – or three pence. The early Brehon laws affirmed the primacy of fire and when Patrick lit the fire on this peak here, so that the flames might be seen in Tara, he was using the language and authority of fire to reclaim Ireland for God. He was telling the Druids to pack up their curses and mistletoe and get on home.

From this we can see that imaginative power was the real power then; it was the imagination which made the statement and, if this statement was strong and powerful enough, then it became victorious. Patrick had always used the powerful workings of his imagination to rout demons and fight his enemies. Any enduring or important changes are always fashioned by the simple powers of the mind. Always. Look at what Jesus managed to achieve with his strong mind. The life and power of the imagination, we may remember, was one of the greatest gifts and original teachings of the Celtic Church.

We walked here after our party had disembarked at Drogheda and Patrick spotted Slane which, as a small matter of detail, is just twelve feet lower than Tara. He told us to build the fire and it took us about a day or so to cart in the dead branches. Patrick himself lit it at dusk, standing in front of it and holding up his crozier, black on flaming red and yellow, telling the king that it was time to row his boat in. The first Easter in Ireland had begun and the Irish were to be released from their terror and fear.

The king was preparing to throw a big party in Tara so he took the timing of our fire very badly indeed. His Druids explained that the fire might even be the fulfilment of long-standing prophecy that his rule was about to end, and that made him even madder. 'Unless this fire is put out tonight the man who lit it will conquer us all,' one soothsayer told him. 'He will overthrow you and make all your subjects his forever.'

The king ordered his soldiers to get over to our camp and drag Patrick before him. They did indeed come crashing in with all the subtlety of a bag of hammers but Patrick managed to convince them that our party would walk over to Tara the next morning unaided.

Almost as soon as we set out the next morning word reached us that some jealous Druids were about to attack us in a country lane. Patrick began chanting the sacred Lorica when we reached the lane and our thirty-strong party was duly changed into a herd of passing deer – a rather lovely doe followed by all her fawns. It fooled the Druids anyway and they didn't interfere with us.

Patrick was still chanting the Lorica when we entered Tara to be presented to the king sitting up high on his throne in the huge Hall of Assembly. This hall was almost as immense as a cathedral, full of sunlight and shadow, possibly the largest building in the world at the time. There were six doors in each of the main walls and they had been left open so the inhabitants of Tara could pack inside and watch us arrive. They did so in complete silence, a whole curious mob of them, many in their white mantles with gold pins but many more in their working clothes. Each had his own particular seat, I was to learn later, and so the west side was allocated to people like cooks, builders, jesters and chess players. Those on

110

the east side were the more arty types like the satirists, flute players, engravers and soothsayers.

But it was the king we had come to meet, and there he was sitting on his throne like the clueless fathead he was, holding a scarlet shield in one hand, a gold collar around his neck and a thick purple cloak over his shoulders. He looked distinctly unamused by us, as did all his warriors who were standing behind the throne, holding up their swords and shields and peering over them at our small singing party. It was the usual pagan way to try and intimidate with a show of military muscle. But Patrick was never intimidated by anyone or anything. Such was his charisma that all he did was just stand there before them and one by one the warriors began to lower their swords and shields and stand to attention respectfully. Patrick's blue-eyed look and long white beard had an almost natural arrogance. We're not going to have any trouble out of you lot, they said.

Then the king wheeled in a gang of his favoured Druids, again in some clear, if hopeless, attempt to intimidate Patrick. These Druids were a pretty clapped-out bunch of cormorants and caterpillars, constantly scraping to the king with their wild long hair and shaking hands. Their main man, dressed in the ritual stained sheet, barely looked as if he could tell one end of a sprig of mistletoe from the other.

But the old duffer conferred with his cronies a lot before stepping forward, muttering some mumbo-jumbo and flicking his fingers in the air when, lo and behold, he actually turned day into night. I was all but speechless with amazement that any human being could do something like that and the king was dancing around in the murk with so much joy that I was reasonably certain he hadn't seen anything like it either. 'So now you must accept that our powers are superior to yours,' the king sneered at Patrick.

111

You could have pulled all Patrick's toenails out and he would never have accepted anything like that. He merely replied: 'All right tell this Druid to restore the light. Show us he can do that.'

Again the old duffer began all his finger-flicking mumbo-jumbo but it remained dark. In fact the Druid stuck at it for half an hour and almost everyone in the hall was shuffling around impatiently. 'Try lighting a candle,' someone shouted from the watching crowd, doubtless one of those satirists. You know how satirists are.

'You see, my king, it is always possible to make darkness,' Patrick said finally. 'But what the world needs today are bringers of light. We need to bask in the glories of the daylight since evil always does its best work in the darkness of the night. Jesus said: "I am the light of the world." And that is the news that I am bringing to you this Easter, my king. The good news of the light of the world.'

Patrick raised his hand and there were gasps as he created the illusion that the sun was rising directly up out of the hall's floor. It was a statement of such raw and passionate power that, one after the other, the warriors laid their swords in front of him, this bringer of a great new light into a world of Druidical darkness. Prophecy had indeed been fulfilled and the king was finally to give Patrick the freedom to preach the word of God in any part of the kingdom he chose.

I left Slane and journeyed the nine miles over to Tara later that day and could just about remember the details of the small jumbled city which once flourished there. It now looks like a crazy golf course although I could make out the site of the Hall of Assembly. Centuries of bad Irish weather had taken their toll on the original contours of the hill and there was evidence of a lot of sporadic fencing and ditching. Some British Israelites had dug into it like a gang of demented moles at the beginning of this century after a rumour had got around that the Ark of the Covenant had been buried here. Modern archaeologists have also made their own rather more controlled investigations but, between the lot of them, they had got it mostly wrong and the original Tara looked nothing at all like the 'intrinsically intelligent' map which stood at the gateway to the site.

Oh sure they had found some jewellery and a few old bones on which they had built their theories – and they had got the site of the Hall of Assembly more or less right. But I do not suppose even the best archaeologists could have got really close to that city which, far from being the 'fair, radiant city of the western world' which the ancient poets were always blithering on about, was in fact quite some dump with all its strange, stinking smells and rickety, wooden houses, its light industry and the variety of its musicality, its mad religious beliefs and the downright cruelty of her warring peoples. All any animal could ever expect in Tara was a good kick.

The tenor of the place was Otherworld. The whole of life was wrapped in a tissue of rituals and omens, in the casting of spells and the following of superstitious practices. Even the enclosures at Tara were not built as a defence against earthly forces; they were defences against magic and the fear of spells so life, such as it was, was but a short journey through a labyrinth of murder and fear. Nothing was pleasant about life in Tara and it was from this that Patrick had come to deliver the people. He even made some notable converts almost as soon as he arrived, but the king never showed any interest in experiencing the transforming love and peace of Christianity – not in his lifetime nor indeed after it. He instructed that he should be buried in his own rath in a standing position and in full armour, facing south – in the direction of his traditional enemy, the men of Leinster. Quite what he hoped to achieve in this mad posture of moribund aggression is difficult to work out, but they were all as mad as March hares.

The other myth that percolated from Tara was that Patrick demonstrated the nature of the Trinity to the king and his people by using the trefoil shamrock. But he did not. Patrick had nothing at all to do with the shamrock and he could not have used it to demonstrate the nature of the Trinity to the assembled people simply because the leaf was too small. Also, while we're on the subject, the shamrock is not special to Ireland and can be found in almost any country in the world.

Today there are a few houses in Tara with a small shop and restaurant run for the tourists. The shop is owned by Dessy Maguire, a man of rude good health who enjoys the chesty crows who have set up a parliament in the trees at the bottom of his garden. 'Ah 'tis grand to hear them so early. They go out to feed at about ten in the morning and come home at about four thirty. There's a small group of them who stay behind to work on the nests and I've noticed that none of them work on Sundays.'

A charabanc pulled up outside his shop and a car drove away. A guide escorted the new group out around the various mounds explaining that this sorry little hillock was the Mound of the Hostages where the king used to incinerate any number of hostages, usually from noted families, to help keep those families in a state of submission.

I do not know where they got all this from, since that mound was nothing less than a small crematorium and the prison block was out on the other side of the hill because the prisoners' cries used to get on the townsfolk's nerves. Nevertheless I kept listening to the guide when I picked up a huge ball of cold air rolling straight across the site. Even the tourists began shivering and chattering with the cold and I turned to see a lone figure standing on top of one of the mounds about a hundred yards away.

I knew that icy cartwheel of air had been directed towards me and it did not take too much longer to work out who she was.

I would bet forty screaballs that the lone figure was the mad blonde I had last seen in St David's. I took a few steps towards her but she was showing no sign of aggression and there was not so much as a glint of a weapon in her hand. She stood there with her hands in her mackintosh pockets. Her long blonde hair was moving around in the breezes but otherwise she remained motionless against a still, blue sky.

'Just over there was the mound of Medb, the old Celtic Queen of Connaught,' the guide was saying, while pointing in the direction of the mad blonde. 'All the old kings of Tara would ritually mate with the voracious Medb and over in Lough Erne we can see statues of similar females. They are always sitting with their knees apart, offering themselves in a constant state of sexual readiness. But few men ever survived Medb's hungry sexuality. She ripped them apart with her perverted, animal passion but, if they did survive her, they became kings. Medb was beautiful but thoroughly evil.'

Well this guide seemed to be able to make his stories fascinating and interesting enough. People's interest always perks up considerably if there is any mention of sex. He was young and wore a denim shirt hanging outside his jeans with a leather pouch slung over his shoulder. There was a sort of pinched earnestness about his face.

'Kings came and went but the kingdom was really controlled by this bitch queen. Anyone hoping to be king had to spend a night with her and, if he didn't satisfy her nymphomaniac needs, she destroyed him.'

Strange and difficult ideas were struggling with one another in my mind and I felt quite sick, unsure whether to stop still or make a quick run for it. The blonde was still there on her hill.

'But even this ice queen could go through the most

fantastic changes, sometimes serene and beautiful but turning into a pure hag with the face of a dribbling pig and a twisted, ugly body. But whether beautiful or ugly she was always violent.'

I frowned and stared hard at the guide before looking over at my own blonde hag who still had not moved and was now smiling.

'You must understand that there is never any future in Ireland,' the guide continued. 'All that ever happens in Ireland is the past over and over again. Every principle of Irish history always remains the same even if they keep turning up in a new disguise. That's all you ever need to understand. The Irish keep making the same mistakes and, when you understand that, you understand us.'

But, funny thing, this guide did not seem to be talking to his party any longer. This guide was talking to me and we both turned to look at the mad blonde on her hillock.

'Remember the old Celtic story of the changeling swans of Lir,' this 'guide' went on, speaking slowly and deliberately like a teacher trying to explain something important to a particularly dim pupil. 'It serves almost as a template for all Irish history. Beautiful children were changed into swans for 300 years before St Mackevig changed them back again. They returned in wrinkled senility but their souls remained beautiful. So it has always been in Ireland. Faces keep changing but, good or evil, their souls always remain the same.'

This guide was trying to tell me something – but I was not sure what – so, almost in exasperation, I strode towards the mad blonde, to squeeze the situation, if only to see what might happen.

What happened was not a lot at first since she remained standing still when, oh blimey, her mackintosh fell apart and I saw that she was going to expose her nakedness to me again.

There was nothing remotely sexually subversive about

116

what she did reveal, as it turned out, since her naked body was a picture of pure ugliness and, when she saw my look of pure horror, she merely cackled loudly showing a long row of black and broken teeth.

All that ever happens in this country is the past over and over again. Could the mad blonde really be the pagan Queen Medb come back in disguise to haunt me? Did all old demons come back as new demons in disguise? Do the principles of evil always stay the same but merely look different? I understood everything and nothing and, in the absence of any sensible alternative, decided to make a run for it, taking off out of Tara and leaping off a high stone wall near the cemetery with Dessy Maguire's crows circling the skies above my head as I ran.

8

Visions of Hell in Ulster

———◦◦———

MORNING BROKE OVER the city and with it came lots of
rain which gushed down on the three main rivers – the
Rhymney, the Ely and the Taff – as they rolled down the
city's main arteries before coming together in a wide flat
basin and flowing out into the bay and the Bristol
Channel. Even this early returning salmon were jumping
in the weir in the Taff in the castle grounds, driven by an
absolute need to be somewhere else, somewhere warm
perhaps and away from all this rain. The windows of
many of the cars were thick with mist as they queued to
get into the city centre.

This was a shower without end as it poured down on
the Celtic capital of Cardiff, washing over the houses in
the outlying suburbs, the roads which ran directly into
the city's heart and over the castle, the National Stadium
and the central pedestrian shopping precinct where the
first of the shoppers under their umbrellas were busy
hunting out bargains as they zipped from one shop doorway to the next. The first of the shoplifters were out
too – as were the store detectives – all stretching and
limbering up for another long day of hide and seek
behind the hosiery and jumper counters.

The splendid Edwardian civic centre was also getting
its share of the rain as it washed over the high, white
Portland stone cliffs of the law courts, the City Hall and
the National Museum. Finding a place to park around
here at this time is always difficult but even more so

today, when everyone wanted to be in their dry cars. A car park attendant with a peaked cap ordered a lady out of the 'private' car park in front of the City Hall and she angrily berated him with a string of unladylike cuss words.

Inside the City Hall – where breathing the hot, still air was as difficult and appetizing as swallowing cough medicine – the dozen white Serreva marble statues of the Heroes of Wales were at least dry as they stood motionless on their plinths in the Marble Hall; they were frozen stiff for all eternity with blank eyes and raised fingers as the civic office workers shuffled past them, barely giving a thought to what the poet Dafydd ap Gwilym or the Bible translator Bishop Morgan or the Celtic warrior chief Owain Glyndwr might have been going on about if, indeed, they went on about anything at all. Outside the building, up on the roof, was a damp, stone dragon, with its mouth forking with cold fire, and an English renaissance clock tower. All of the clock's five bells, made from the finest gun metal and with tunes to give the hours and the Westminster quarters, were dedicated to God.

The rain had managed to hold back the usual numbers of shoppers who were normally milling everywhere by this time on a Saturday morning. Many had already made it to – and were lingering in – the city's fine shopping arcades, their wet shoes sloshing along the walkways as the rain beat ceaselessly and rhythmically on the arcades' glass roofs. Several buskers were at it in some of the arcades, lighting up their chosen porches in small golden explosions of music before the police moved them on again. The pubs were not yet serving, although a few of the thirsty were gathering patiently outside the locked doors of the Old Arcade, waiting for that magical shift of several iron bolts which meant that their thirst would soon be over. There were some strange people here too, including One O'Clock John who always screamed out – no matter where he was – at the stroke of One O'Clock;

119

Nobby with all his possessions in a supermarket trolley; and Billy Bostick, the glue sniffer.

Next to the Old Arcade was the central market, a place of crowded stalls and dizzying pongs, of sawdust floors and piled-up meat, of vegetables and biscuits and puppies sitting in glass cages waiting for some softie to take them home. There were record stalls and sweet counters and little cafés with but three seats where the faggots and peas were as good as anywhere in the world. Pigeons burbled ceaselessly in the eaves, doubtless wondering if the morning might ever dry up enough so they could get out and forage for food in the streets. Pigeons hate the rain too.

Down at the start of Bute Street and the entrance to the docks girls in high heels clattered along the pavement, underneath the iron railway bridge, as the trains rumbled loudly and ominously overhead. This bridge marked the start of old Tiger Bay – except there is little tigerish about the bay in such rain. The working girls were not yet out and about outside the Custom House Hotel – because rain is always bad for business – and, this being Saturday, lots of the offices were closed down there, although a horse and cart was going about some mysterious business to do with scrap iron. Raindrops hit into puddles just outside the Greek Orthodox church and the nearby Anglican church. Down a few blocks again was the Moslem mosque where, no matter what the weather, they were always hard at their morning prayers with their shoes left in neat, polished lines outside.

Elsewhere nothing moved in Bute Street except the cold flights of rain all the way down to the dockland itself. This was once the largest coal exporting city in the world, but is now busy reinventing itself as a commercial centre with lots of new houses, a County Hall which looks like a Chinese pagoda in disguise, and lots of other grand plans for buildings like grand opera houses for which they cannot yet find an appropriately grand sum of

120

money. But the new Harry Ramsden's fish and chip restaurant on the Pier Head, with all its glittering chandeliers, looked smart enough in the rain with a reasonable menu too at £6.80 for cod and chips together with a pot of tea and bread and butter. Who needs a grand opera house when you can sit down to a nice plate of cod and chips?

Way across the Bristol Channel a horizontal streak of bright sunlight on the English side was just about managing to cut in beneath the low, black rain clouds. Soon this sunlight would probably manage to lift these rain clouds higher and yet higher, making them break up so that the sun could shine down again on this fine and gracious city of Cardiff which I have always, even in my blackest moments of exhaustion and doubt, loved passionately and without reservation.

Bright, cold sunshine was swarming down on Edinburgh, the Athens of the North, all strung out around the three principal streets of Princes Street, George Street and Queen Street and scattered around the high castle on a rock, where they still fire guns on the Queen's birthday. Not that such sunshine suited Auld Reekie all that well, since it managed to highlight many of the blemishes on the houses, particularly their sootied state, never having been cleaned up after the age of the coal fire.

But there was a singing jubilation in these sunny streets this lunchtime because Welsh supporters, with their red and white scarves and rattles, had invaded this Scottish stronghold for their annual set-to in rugby, a game which is always engaged fiercely with a real Celtic passion. So there was a bigger uproar than usual around the Sir Walter Scott Memorial, John Knox's old house, and the various other bopping bistros and pubs. The sounds of duelling bagpipes rose into the air as big men in kilts joshed with little men carrying giant leeks and

121

others went scuttling around feverishly looking for a spare ticket, and yet more mounted the bonnets of cars or hung off lamp-posts shouting: 'Oggey-oggey-oggey.' 'Oi, oi, oi.'

You could not swing the smallest mouse in any of the crowded bars as the malt mixed with the heavy and the air was thick with the cracked lilt of several competing choirs. There is always a fine sense of singing fellowship when the Celtic tribes meet; never any sense of nastiness or fisticuffs which so often springs up when the Anglo-Saxon tribe hits town. This is one of the greatest cities of them all to get drunk in, although there will be some very sad scenes later this night when, win or lose, both tribes will be out for the count and, more often than not, crashlanded in gutters or throwing up all over the place.

In Princes Street the pavements were becoming even more fevered with singing gangs from Ferndale falling into the arms of singing gangs from Inverness. There were the hot dog salesmen, the aggressive sellers of the *Big Issue* and, almost inevitably, a milkcrate messiah outside a chip shop, with voice raised and finger prodding the sky, warning all and sundry of the unpleasant and dire consequences unless they repent – and repent now.

Two policemen stood in front of this milkcrate messiah outside the chip shop and warned him to keep his voice down. But he was not having any of that. Oh no. He didn't care if they ran him in. Anyway he couldn't keep his voice down even if he wanted to since, whenever he spoke it was always in the Holy Spirit and, if the Holy Spirit wanted it loud, then loud it had to be. There was simply nothing he could do about it. So stick that up your kilt. Perhaps predictably, the policemen did not understand the needs, desires or powers of the Holy Spirit so they merely left him to rant on as loudly as he wanted on his milkcrate outside the chip shop.

As kick-off time approached, the singing gangs began making their way to Murrayfield by any means available, including their own two tottering feet. There they were going to re-enact the tribal disputes of old on the terraces even if, for the Welsh, this was not just an old tribal fight but also a form of worship. The Welsh would be singing from the hymnsheet of William Williams of Pantycelyn whose hymn, 'Guide me, oh Thou Great Jehovah', with its repeated refrain of 'Feed me 'til I want no more', was nothing less than a collective Welsh plea to be fed with the bread of heaven of an incredible number of points; the more the better.

This game of rugby has always had a strange place in the Celtic psyche, particularly when you consider that it was learned from the playing fields of the English public school. Here was a way, the modern Celts decided, in which they could take on the English at their own game and, with a bit of luck and a fair breeze, beat the hell out of them. Here was a game in which they could exact revenge for centuries of English wrong-doing; a game in which, both in defence and attack, they could relive old battles against the hated Saxons and Normans in their big, damp castles.

They were not taking on the English today, unfortunately, but one another, although the atmosphere was as tense as ever as the two sides ran out into the cold Murrayfield sunshine. Flags flew and huge spasms of emotion rolled around the packed crowds. Hymns mixed with arias as two imaginative and passionate tribes prepared to engage in a series of imaginative and passionate responses to a long and bloody struggle. The kick-off whistle blew and a huge, multi-voiced roar went up as the duly anointed representatives of both tribes, in their respective red and blue colours, duly got down to the matter of punching the lights out of one another over the frantically disputed possession of a funny shaped ball.

It was cold and dark as I got into Belfast on the night in

question and I was feeling unbearably tense. There were no crowds, sunshine or rain as I moved about the city, just the dark and the cool of the end of my journey. A strange sound lifted up out of the city darkness. It was a long, low moan of sorrow which, sometimes soft and sometimes hard, just kept going on and on. The sound of weeping seemed to wrap itself around this sorrowing moan when everything fell silent again.

A lone seagull fluttered down into the thin yellow glow of the street lamp and hung there, crying out to me, loudly and piercingly, as if locked in some prolonged torment. The still and shuttered houses along the Falls Road also carried huge burdens of suffering. Winds cried deep in their aching chimney breasts as the odd cloud moved across a bright, starry sky. The cleated boots of an Army patrol with guns and faces blackened walked past. Almost directly overhead a helicopter was whump-whumping with its searchlight spinning over the rooftops. Way out on the other side of the city were the black crucifix shapes of the Harland and Woolf shipyard and, further out again, low black hills surrounding a darkly glittering sea lough.

A small shop had caught fire in one side-road and I caught the outlines of two muscular, semi-naked men in the flickering fire light. One had sunglasses and was sitting astride a motorcycle. The other had what looked like a flame-thrower in his hands and I was pretty sure he was that man I had last seen shouting about Dunblane on the Isle of Skye. A sort of yowling came from a distance and the pair took off fast on the motorcycle.

A huge pack of dogs came running down the road who looked like those Liffey dogs and were certainly making the same sort of noise as they snapped and snarled at one another. Occasionally they stopped to fight before running on again, anxious to get close to the fire and sniff around the charred shell of the shop.

I moved off smartly into the night, passing the lurid

graffiti on the walls and end-of-terrace murals of armalites and balaclavaed warriors. Every small opening seemed to be grilled or smothered with barbed wire. Shards of glass were embedded in cement on the tops of walls and I spotted the odd defeated face looking out into the road. This was the age of lawlessness all right. Down on the next corner I picked up that sound of heartbreaking sorrow again, a whole wave breaking over my head and making me want to cry out too.

Another camera locked on me and I knew that every step I took was being photographed. This government spies on our every move and hiccup. Those dishes on the side of the police station will be listening to every conversation; those cameras will be recording the delivery of every tradesman to every home; the amounts of every electricity and gas bill will be monitored on some internal computer and checked for every inexplicable variation. This is a country where the mail is always first read by someone other than to whom it is addressed. All telephone calls are routinely tapped.

But if you really want to know what has happened in this city for the past thirty years study her walls. There were new walls, ruined walls and walls covered with murals. Masked men with rocket launchers featured in a lot of the murals, although more significant than these walls were the so-called peace walls: architect-designed metal walls just that little bit too high so that no one can heave a petrol bomb over them late on a Saturday night. Everyone now needs a wall to tell them where they may and may not go. These are tribal fences which mark out the boundaries of the mind. That low moan of sorrow again.

I had walked near Milltown cemetery on the Falls when there was a flash of light striking glass and my blood froze when Balor stepped out onto the pavement in front of me. He was holding his spear but there was none of the imagery of old in the huge lens of his eye, just all kinds of lights which kept flashing and making his eye enlarge or shrink at will. It was a strange trick and I could not think what he was trying to do when the lights in his eye went off with a loud click. Then he turned and shone a thin beam of brilliant white light on a tombstone in the cemetery.

A man materialized behind the tombstone wearing a flat cap, a blue anorak and black boots. He had a thick face with long, straggly hair and a goatee beard, and was clearly up to no good, because he opened his anorak and began taking out some grenades from the blue denim pouches he had strapped around his chest. Then, rather pointedly, he pulled the pins on the grenades and lobbed them straight at me. At me! The grenades exploded with loud bangs and the night was full of drifting smoke and ricocheting bits of tombstone, but I stayed rooted in my terror. Next the gunman took out an automatic pistol and began firing directly at me. *Wham, wham, wham.*

It was soon clear that neither the gunman nor Balor could actually hurt me physically, so I managed to overcome my terror and decided the best thing I could do was leg it out of the Falls as fast as I could.

I took to the night running but became vaguely aware that Balor was tracking me. There were a few more explosions with bullets slamming into the walls around me, when I skidded to a halt and threw up my hands in horror, as Balor's white light had picked up some poor young girl tied to a lamppost after having her head shaved and her body tarred and feathered. She cried piteously but, when I took a few steps towards her, she disappeared into thin air.

I turned and turned again before running on up the Falls when another white light picked up a bleeding body being stretchered into an ambulance. When the ambulance drove away the white light picked up the red bloodstains spattered over the pavement. I backed away in mounting fear, turning into a side-street, when the white light picked up a traffic block manned by men with guns and wearing balaclavas. That deadly white light then picked out a riot with drifting waves of CS gas going this way and that.

All these flashing images undermined my basic functions. I could not even run properly and kept whirling around and around trapped in my own fear. Even my own pursuing shadow made me jump. I did manage to evade the road block by doubling back through a garden which, in turn, brought me to the Falls where I was accompanied by the continual plunk-plunking of my own frightened heart.

It stayed quiet for a while as I reached the end of the road near the city centre and I even heard the sound of chinking glasses and laughter coming from a party. Oh I could do with a good party just now, I thought, as I passed under the arches of a new motorway system and crossed over a huge patch of wasteland. A yellow taxi pulled up about twenty yards away from me and I noticed the taxi driver was just sitting in his cab and watching me. I ignored him and crossed the site of some old factory where the ground was littered with rubble and broken glass.

I knew that I was in trouble again when I saw the taxi was circling the site and almost certainly tailing me. When I crossed the next road, he seemed to accelerate out of nowhere and stop near me, flashing his headlamps at me twice. This was no ordinary taxi driver out looking for a late night fare. That much was clear. This might even be another old demon intent on starting trouble, out looking for a fight.

He was getting out of his cab and I turned to face him when . . . oh no . . . this one began unbuttoning his olive drab field jacket and, as it fell apart, it revealed an enormous array of knives and guns strapped to his chest. This man was a walking arsenal and, now that I was standing at a certain angle to his headlamps, I saw he had one of those tight, psychotic smiles. His eyes were also slyly piggy but, even more strangely, he had shaved his head except for a single strip of hair in the style of a Mohican.

This one was born to raise hell and I knew that I was in deep trouble when he advanced towards me, firing off shots at me with a pistol in each hand. But, again strange to report, I did not actually seem to be hurt by his bullets even if I was as frightened as a threatened puppy as I took off again into that dark and doomed Belfast night.

I was passing a cluster of trees and heading towards the Shankhill when there was a sudden roar of sorrow as I crossed the road and I was literally run over by a long funeral procession. I was forced to lie in the middle of the road as this procession walked through me and there did not seem any end to it. Mourners followed hearses and yet more mourners followed yet more hearses, all walking quietly, some carrying wreaths and others supporting broken, weeping widows. I tried to get up but could not. It was almost as if I was being pinned down right there in the middle of the road by a nation's grief. Even breathing was difficult as they kept tramping through me.

There might have been thousands of mourners and, as I remained there, I noticed with mounting alarm that their heads were covered with halos of blood. But then something stranger happened since their clothes began to disintegrate and, where they were once burnished in their Sunday best, they were now in tatters – long, pitiful strips of rag. Barefoot, they stumbled painfully after each hearse. These mourners were nothing but skin and bones, and it was almost as if they were struggling to the cemetery not to bury whoever the hearses were carrying but themselves. All their mouths were green.

This funeral without end was connected with the old

days of the famine, I knew, and I doubt I had ever experienced such levels of pure suffering as when it continued to move through me.

I squeezed my eyes shut and cried out, unable to stand this hallucinating torture any further when, almost as quickly as it had come, the funeral procession disappeared and I found myself still lying in the middle of the road staring towards the Shankhill. There was no movement in the surrounding houses. No parties, no laughter, no nothing . . .

Yes there actually was a direct link between the nature of the famine of old and the Troubles of today. They both had a fungus at their rotten hearts, the one biological and the other technological. Where one needed a few diseased potato tubers to get going, this one only needed a handful of sick psychopaths. Where one needed lots of rain to germinate, the other needed a hot summer suitable for street riots. Where one fungus had the fantastic ability to multiply into thousands and thousands of deadly zoospores in the right conditions, then so, too, the terrorist, in the fertilizing heat of publicity, which he craves and needs, can also release thousands and thousands of deadly zoospores of violence and fear through electronic circuits. These, in their turn, set up a widespread nucleus of infection which trickles into every home and arrives on every hearth attacking all who sit there while also fomenting violence, undermining faith and the healthy tissues of the family. These technological zoospores, which had been hatched inside a fungus of corruption and which, as in the days of the famine, kept insisting they were an effect and not a cause, were now eating at the very heart and mind and spirit of God.

And remember, my people, the fungus of corruption always – *but always* – comes first. You do indeed keep making the same mistakes and coming up with the same results. So how long now – and how many more are going to die – until you finally understand that the fungus of corruption – this fungus which keeps insisting that it's not even there – really is there and that it always, without fail, comes first?

It was late and I was getting tired as I trudged up the Shankhill. Bellicose Union Jacks fluttered wanly in the night breeze and the kerb stones were painted red, white and blue. Every corner had a burned-out car or a bricked-up building with whole areas fenced in by barbed wire and metal sheets. STUFF THE FENIANS. UP THE BRITS. NO SURRENDER.

I heard that moan of sorrow again and picked up a few metallic noises. My long night of fear was far from over, I saw. Something else was about to happen although I could hardly have foreseen what since, just at that moment, the Shankhill street lamps got brighter and I noticed a short spurt of fire coming from a television aerial on one of the rooftops. A television aerial!

I heard a bang and spotted another spurt of fire when a bullet cracked into the ground next to me. I moved forward carefully when there was yet another fusillade of fiery spurts and sharp bangs. I stopped still for a while, choking on my own astonishment: television aerials just don't fire shots at you. Then something even more improbable happened. All the satellite dishes were turning their fat faces towards me and they too began firing, hitting the ground and walls around me with bullets so big they were punching holes the size of fists in the tarmac. One even winged me and I reached to put a hand on the moon to steady myself when, as suddenly as the attack had started, it ended, leaving me shaking like a jelly in the wind and hanging on to the moon for dear life.

Right. That was it. I was out of here and straight back to my hotel and bed.

I was, I suppose, about half a mile away from my hotel

when a bomb exploded, somewhere near the business district around Donegal Square. Shock waves kept surging through the city streets and I turned one corner to peer down a long avenue where I saw, in the distance, an erupting pillar of fire with disturbed birds flying all around it.

I walked towards the fire as the dogs of the Liffey came tearing around the corner, sweeping me off my feet as they went snarling and yapping their way towards the explosion. My Lord they were an unkempt, scabby bunch, at times busier fighting with one another than actually getting to the scene of the explosion. Why did they always seem to be in such a primeval fury to get there first? I mean what would they miss if they were a second or two behind everyone else?

A curious stillness had settled on the night by the time I reached the fire which was spreading from one house to the next. A man who had lost both his legs was dragged from one house and the dogs sniffed around his bleeding stumps curiously but with no real interest when another body was dragged out and another. Later the fires had spread further and the dogs were sitting back on their haunches, baying to the flames in a surreal rapture.

I felt I was drowning in the city's tears. I could not make any sense of it when I looked up and saw things were far worse than I had imagined. The city birds had long since flown and about three dozen dark angels, attracted by the explosion and the howling dogs, were now circling the skies above the fire. With their huge wings spread wide they were going round and round like giant vultures waiting on death.

I looked towards the other side of the city and saw an enormous dark angel, carrying a huge bag in his talons, coming in low over the Harland and Woolf shipyard. When he came close he drove his wings backwards hard which kept him suspended in the air as he shook out the contents of his bag over the fire. It was difficult to see what he was shaking – they seemed like small rocks which hit the fire with soft, yellow explosions. The other circling dark angels, each in turn, swooped straight down into the fire and picked up one of these fiery rocks before powering out to the city suburbs. They flew for a while, with these small clumps of fire in their talons, before dropping them off in outlying areas where they, in turn, ignited yet more fires. The dogs kept salivating and howling their approval at these fiery flights.

Within the space of two minutes the first fire caused by the bomb blast had now spread to a dozen or more parts of the city. It could have been one of those destructive firestorms started by the British bombers in World War II as the dark angels kept flying their sorties and dropping their flaming payloads before turning around and flying back to pick up more. The silhouettes of frightened, tortured people kept running through the flames as explosion followed explosion. The Ardoyne, the Shankhill, the Falls, Ballymurphy . . . yellow and red explosions of flame tore through roof after roof as people frantically loaded up their handcarts to run to the relative safety of the countryside. Almost everyone wanted to escape this spreading firestorm, with the whole city sinking beneath a waving field of fire, except there was no escape because no sooner had they passed through one field of flames than they faced another.

Not that the fires were confined to the city, since I spotted more than a few dark angels carrying their payloads outside the city and dropping them in the province at large.

Oh my poor people of Ulster what is happening to you? What are they doing to you?

I kept raising my hands in gestures of helplessness and there were all kinds of voices joggling together in my mind; voices, perhaps, from my own Celtic past when one voice rose up into this fire-filled night of dark angels: 'So he has come then and is engulfing the world,' Evan

Roberts called out right along the length of the century. His voice, as usual, was jubilant with prophecy and deadly with the revelation of his words. 'Lucifer and all his dark angels have finally escaped their dungeon in hell and are even now preparing themselves for the last desperate rebellion against God. Beware my people. Arm yourselves with holiness because this hurricane of evil will tear you apart in ways that you don't understand. This force will come as organized intelligence scattering illusions at your feet. It will even be anxious to tell you that Satan does not exist. But he does, my people, and he is even now throwing a cloak of violence and perversion all over the face of the world.'

Well I'd had enough and walked slowly and sadly back to my hotel; a confused and defeated Gulliver who had found himself shipwrecked on some wild and distant Celtic shore; a man who had come to the Emerald Isle looking for the old Celtic glory but who had ended up learning something of the nature of modern Celtic evil.

And as I continued walking I noticed that almost all the demons were out in the Belfast streets taking the night air. They were chatting on street corners or calling out to one another, evidently unconcerned about my existence, if they had noticed me at all. The huge and brilliant lens of Balor was strolling up the pavement, with his funny metallic legs, and, on the other side of the road, the mad blonde was talking to the muscular motorcyclist with sunglasses. The Mohican was standing beneath the light of the next lamp-post cleaning his fingernails with a knife and talking manically to himself.

There were some new ones around too since, further on again, there were five men in sharp suits, white shirts, black ties and sunglasses, all trooping down the pavement together as they fiddled with their jackets. A young man with a completely shaven head, blue sunglasses and carrying a pump-action shotgun, accompanied by a young girl, walked up to the five men and they began cussing loudly and obscenely, with the young man even breaking his gun as if in readiness to shoot the five men.

On the next corner was a really strange type: a man with nails sticking out of his head. I heard some noises and turned to see a man standing inside a shop window and tapping the glass trying to get my attention. His face looked as if he had been freshly dug up and he wore an old homburg. But, somewhat oddly, his fingernails, with which he was tapping the glass, were long and metallic.

I might have been St Patrick chanting his Lorica as he walked through the crowded Hall of Assembly up to the king at Tara. Certainly I felt close to God as I continued, trusting in his ability to look after me in the face of this massing evil.

It has to be said this lot no longer bothered me any more than I them. They were nasty illusions, I kept telling myself, who could never hurt me as long as I stayed away from them. They were just old demons masquerading in new clothes, who would get their comeuppance when God decided he was ready to purge them. Then there were the dogs of the Liffey to deal with even if the dark angels might take a little longer.

That sorrowing sound came again, a cry of pain from the past made new, and I knew who it was. It was Deirdre, the daughter of King Conor's story-teller at Navan who fell in love with a young man and ran away with him and his two brothers to Scotland. The king pleaded with them to return and, when they did, he had the three young men killed. Deirdre was heartbroken and, for a whole year, never laughed or so much as smiled or raised her head.

Finally the king gave her away in a forced marriage and, as she was leaving Navan in a chariot, she let out a long cry before leaping off the chariot and killing herself by breaking her head on a rock. The earth swallowed her body and a yew tree grew out of her grave. The branches spread across the country until they found the branches of another yew which grew out of her lover's grave.

This became the great archway of Deirdre of the Sorrows and, all these years later, Deirdre was still crying for those that she had loved and lost.

It would be nice and even convenient if I could have ended my Belfast night of terror – and my investigation into the Celtic Heart – with the story of Deirdre. But it did not quite work out like that since, as I was walking past the City Hall, I picked up a lot of alien and even rat-like noises coming out of the darkness.

On closer inspection I could see lots of small faces – whole rows of them – and it was not clear what they were doing there either. I went closer, picking up stray whiffs of rough cider until I saw these were local children on a night out, many of them sitting there, each clutching and swigging on flagons of cider. The truly appalling feature of this particular party was that not one of them looked over the age of eleven. They were babies who had not long been walking but were now crawling drunkenly around the walls of the City Hall and making animal noises.

Four of them got up and ran down the side of the building towards another gang also encamped with cider bottles in the distant darkness. Empty bottles were thrown around and a lot of crude cussing before the four returned to their own group where an argument broke out about who had finished the last of the cider. Another produced something which looked like a small gas cylinder and they took it in turns to sniff on that a few times before they became drowsy and incoherent.

These were the war babies, the orphans of thirty years of street fighting about nothing at all. These were the kids whose lives had been stolen from them by all the

135

gathered demons, dogs and dark angels who had built this new pagan kingdom of murder and fear. These were the children of the terrorist bullets which would keep travelling forever; the lost children of Balor and a nation which, not for the first time, went to sleep while evil flourished.

It was a tired Gulliver who went home to Wales the following afternoon; a worried and perplexed Gulliver who had seen visions he had not wanted to see and learned things about the rise and fall of the Celt he had not wanted to learn. We Celts please and dismay God in about equal proportions. We promise much with our passion and beautiful ideals, but then lose our way in the charred and smoking fields of our own making.

But, for the Celt, there is an answer to this mess which is uniquely Celtic. We should duly revive the values of the Celtic Heart, become passionate and proud again, relearn the delights of music, poetry and story-telling on the sacred hearth. We should rediscover that huge and deadly sword of the pure imagination and wield it, in our art, against the many enemies of God.

A revived Celtic Heart would put us back into a simple personal relationship with God; it would put women in their rightful place next to men; it would cherish our children and love them avidly. The old Celt understood the sanctity of life and the sacred interconnectedness between everything. He knew exactly how Columba felt when the old saint said: 'I would rather face all the horrors of hell than listen to the sound of an axe being taken to an oak.'

The Celts understood the importance of the purity of water; they believed in the reality of angels as messengers and agents of a dynamic and creative God who watched over the faithful. The Celtic mind accepted the reality of visions; it understood all too clearly that the language of

God was not necessarily our language. His thoughts and ideas were not necessarily our thoughts and ideas. Visions were, then, forms of communication between God and human beings and, sometimes, between human beings themselves. They were ways of talking about God's ideas – even his feelings – without spelling it out in the banality of language.

A return to the old Celtic standards would do nothing less than purge the violence and viciousness which have bedevilled Ulster for so long. It would simply remove the self-imposed barriers between the warring tribes where, we might remember, *all* the Irish have been the caring sons and daughters of Patrick who, in his turn, cared about them all equally, be they the children of the Reformation or of Rome. The conflict has often been promoted as a religious conflict when nothing could be less likely. This conflict has been continually stirred by demons, dark angels and dogs who have confused and frightened the people while insisting they are not even there. These foul demons would be destroyed and made redundant by a return to the early Celtic colours.

The old Celtic values are timeless and even more relevant now than when they were introduced into a world of murder, superstition and fear back in the fifth century. Celtic values, in which there is not a trace of division or sectarianism, are beyond improvement, no matter how much they might be tampered with – or even ultimately disenfranchised. When – and if – we rediscover them we will be given the intellectual weaponry to become true pilgrims; we will again become a faithful, decent people living happily and peacefully with one another at the foot of the Cross.

The Celtic Heart is brave and strong. It stands for what we are and where we came from and it is the very light by which we can again become safe and secure in this growing darkness. Draw close to it, my people. Cup a hand to your ear and listen for its deathless beat. The

Celtic Heart may even represent our last chance of drawing back from the final hours in which we will perish.

So I have, finally, come to the end of my trail but, try as I might, I still cannot rid my mind of those lost babies swigging cider outside Belfast's City Hall. So as I sit here, choosing my closing words, I would like to conclude by saying it is to those children – and all the other children of our lost and battered Celtic tribes – that this book is hopefully and prayerfully dedicated.